Ireland Beautiful

Ireland Beautiful

BY
WALLACE NUTTING
Author of the States Beautiful Series, etc.

ILLUSTRATED BY THE AUTHOR WITH THREE
HUNDRED AND FOUR PICTURES COVERING
ALL THE COUNTIES IN IRELAND

Bonanza Books · New York

FOREWORD

THERE are, at this writing, no current guide books on Ireland, though two great houses are engaged on editions. This volume pretends to no place as a guide book, nor is its text intended as a serious effort to cover with precision or fullness any part of Ireland. It is merely a record of impressions of beauty or quaintness, observed in a land which for romance and pathos, strange history and legend, for witching grace and mystery, is probably unsurpassed.

Its insularity, climate, uniqueness of feature, its joys, its very misfortunes, attract us, and combine to produce a cumulative effect upon the emotional, the esthetic and the romantic sense. The thought of Ireland, to one who knows anything either of its history or its contour, is accompanied by a tingle and a thrill. It appeals to all our being. We all love her, deplore her, hope for her, and smile with her. Ireland is always interesting, sometimes awful, usually beautiful, and whatever the strangeness of her vicissitudes, her future is the most beautiful and hopeful of our dreams.

A book of wonderful beauty, called " Picturesque Ireland," was published in the middle of the last century. For merit and variety of illustration it surpasses any other single volume I know, on any country whatever. The rare skill and intelligence displayed in that superb work inspired me to attempt, however humbly, to record something for the present generations. The taste and richness of that volume are far beyond me.

All the pictures for half-tone engravings in this volume have been made by me personally in Ireland since the Free State came into being. They at least have the merit of being original, and I may hope, since they cover about seven thousand miles of Irish travel in every one of the thirty-two counties, that they will bring to light and to the attention of others various nooks and corners of Ireland hitherto unknown. This must inevitably be the case, since in many instances I have not followed the beaten track. Most of the famous beauty spots of Ireland are shown. More than half of the illustrations, however, are of the humble cottage life, or of the little streams or coves which are often counted not sufficiently important for artistic rendering. It is just such subjects that appeal to me, and, in my experience, to the public also. No one wants a picture of Niagara Falls, however wonderful and beautiful it may be. I do not say that this is the proper attitude, but I merely state the undoubted fact. I therefore omit some of the more trite themes and this is probably the only volume on record having to do with Ireland that does not include a picture of a jaunting car.

I wish to record my gratitude to the unnumbered friends who have assisted me. The courtesy of hundreds of persons, whose very names I do not know, has been of great help. Bishop Murray, of Portland, at much pains provided me with many important letters. I found, however, that on reaching Ireland it was merely necessary to say that I was an American to secure an *entree* anywhere.

It will be readily understood that the exigencies of the weather or the time of day have caused a fuller showing of some parts of Ireland than others. Several books like this could be prepared not trenching at all upon one another. We are here for today. If we are given tomorrow, possibly another attempt will be made, with altogether new material, but that, if ever, will be years in the future.

I would like to bear witness here that I have found in every portion of Ireland a largeness of spirit towards strangers, irrespective of creed, which gave me a sense of being at home. Were I banished from America today, I think that Ireland would have higher claims upon my regard than any other foreign land.

WALLACE NUTTING

Framingham, Massachusetts
October, 1925

To

THOSE AMERICANS

WHO, FROM BIRTH, HAVE LOVED
OR WHO HAVE LEARNED TO LOVE
OLD IRELAND

Ireland Beautiful

. .
.

IRELAND

IT IS not an overstatement that Ireland is at once the most beautiful and the least known portion of the civilized world. Insularity always makes for solidarity of thought. Insular people are always patriotic. This has been proven in a marvelous way by the settlements made from time to time in Ireland from England, in order to establish a population favorable to English government. More often than not Protestant and Catholic, after a generation or two on the soil, have become intensely Irish. There is a trigness and snugness about an island which gives a dweller on it the sense that it is his own section of Eden. Nature has so sharply marked its bounds that there is no question of their blending with those of another country.. The abruptness of the island as border land leaves no room for dispute.

The reaction of this fact upon admiration of scenery is naturally direct. The island is much like a dwelling in that the inhabitants of each consider their own little domain with its peculiarities, its merits, its beauties, as a part of their own being. The Irishman, naturally loving his island best, thinks his mountains are more impressive, his meadows more fair, than are to be found elsewhere. This is true, because he knows their beauties better than do strangers. This is an agreeable trait of human nature and adds very much to the joy of life. It is not an accident, but something deep in the nature of our being, that when we are at all generous, or even good humored, we tend to see the best in those that are nearest us.

7

When the natural beauties of Ireland are emphasized to the Irish by their insularity, we can easily understand the intensity of the love which the native of Erin has for his isle. It is sometimes used as a reproach against the Irishman, as well as the Scotchman, that he has so much to say in favor of his country, and yet leaves it. The necessity of providing for their own often sends men to the corners of the earth. We have no doubt that if the Irishman had felt there were as good opportunities in his own land as elsewhere, he would have remained there. It is difficult to live on scenery, though certain American states come near doing that, and Switzerland is a standing example of success in that particular.

We do not know why it is that people go so little to Ireland. For the most part, of course, people who go from America abroad follow the beaten track. It is an added expense to detour. Ireland in this respect shares with Spain and some other regions the supposed disadvantage of being off the main line of traffic. The Mediterranean steamers, it is true, have put Spain on the main highway of the nations. The American steamers, however, which touch at Queenstown will not put off freight there, and the writer was under the necessity of taking his motor-car first to Liverpool. This is a hardship which the Irish people should seek to eliminate, and we have no doubt they will find means of overcoming it.

The supposed lack of adequate accommodations for tourists in the remoter parts of Ireland has doubtless caused hesitancy on the part of many about journeying in the island. The absence of great cities in the west of Ireland has not hindered the establishment of accommodations for tourists.

We are apprehensive that the traveler who goes for scenery alone is an exceedingly rare individual. The antiquarian and the poet, the religious person and the historian, find an immense interest in Ireland. These also are exceptional people. Making the grand tour because others have done so is the usual proceeding.

It is to the advantage of the traveler in Ireland that he is not jostled by other sightseers. This advantage almost compensates for the slight inevitable annoyances where travelers seldom go.

American travelers may easily land at Queenstown, and those who, or whose fathers, came from Ireland, will naturally do so. The run across St. George's Channel, is, however, so short that after all reasons are taken account of, we arrive at the decision that there is no sufficient reason why the traveler to Ireland should not be multiplied a hundred fold. One may also land at Londonderry or Belfast, coming from America.

The popularity of Scotland is due to a vast extent to Walter Scott. His influence was enough at least to start thoughtful and reading people northward. Once the vogue was established, there was enough intrinsic merit in the attractions of Scotland to hold steadily the tide of travel going in that direction.

While the Irish are a poetical and romantic people, no one writer among them, certainly not a writer of fiction, has had the popularity of Scott. Swift and Moore, especially the latter, have made men think of Ireland. It is pretty generally known, however, that Swift was eager to get away. "The Bells of Shandon" has done more for making the beauties of Ireland known than any other composition of similar length. There is such a haunting rhythm in the poem, and such an obvious intensity of love expressed for the theme by its writer, that every man with a particle of imagination who reads the poem must almost wish that he had been born an Irishman.

Ireland is the westernmost overture of Europe to America. It has one or two places of which it is jocosely said that the next town on the west is Boston. An increase in commerce or in the tide of travel to Ireland would make it the first, and in some cases, the most important land for transatlantic steamers. The time has been when Galway was a center for world shipping. Bantry Bay, at once wonderful in beauty and in spaciousness, might easily, in process of another century, become a great shipping center.

At the present time, for reasons some of which may be surmised, while others are mysterious, the Irish are not a seafaring people. We find that where they have devoted themselves to fishing, the pinch of poverty has

[*Text continued on page 19.*]

A PATH OF ROSES

In the rose-sweet hush
Of a new day's birth
When dawn's first flush
Is filling the sky
And the dew-washed earth
Where petals lie,
Cool in the morning,
Thatched roofs adorning,
Soft roses press
A perfumed caress
Against snow-white walls,
Bending their stems
Like great velvet balls
Laden with gems —
A dipping, dripping burden of beauty.

But in the hushes
Of ended day
When distant thrushes
Are singing their lay
With the cooing cushat dove;
When heaven above
Is a goblet of wine,
And the glistening vine
Lifts chalices high
To be filled with the sky,
Round cups of rose-mist,
Amber-and-gold-kissed,
Fragrant and frail,
Awaiting the moon
With her white slumber-veil —
O roses of June,
'Tis then that you whisper of love's tender beauty.

Mildred Hobbs

THE PATH OF ROSES—COUNTY GALWAY

THE OVOCA—COUNTY WICKLOW

THE HAUNT OF THE THRUSH—COUNTY CORK

THE PLEASANT LEE—COUNTY CORK

WHERE FAIRIES BATHE—CROOKSTON, COUNTY CORK

A FAMILY BOWER—CONG, COUNTY SLIGO

A LITTLE BAY—NEAR GLENGARIFF

AN UNDER MOUNTAIN COTTAGE—COUNTY DOWN

A WESTPORT GARDEN

CASTLE AND ABBEY—ADARE

KINSALE HARBOR—COUNTY CORK

BLACKWATER BRIDGE—COUNTY KERRY

been felt in recent years to a greater extent than in any other calling in Ireland.   Until recently the demands of English trade have discouraged by legal means the development of an Irish marine.   Possibly the doing away with that handicap may in time stimulate the Irish to become a sea-faring people, and various ports in Ireland, as Wexford, Waterford, Dublin, and Limerick, were settled by the Danes, the people who as Vikings symbolized early contests with and victories over the sea.   So true is this, that the Vikings were thought of almost as amphibious.

After they had become settled on the soil, however, they seem to have abandoned the sea for the most part.   Hence, for one reason or another, this outmost post of Europe, fertile, abounding in wonderful harbors and contiguous to the best fishing grounds, has neither seized the trident nor placed the crown of Neptune on its head.   The contrast between the marine development of England and Ireland is one of the curious phenomena of history.

It may very well be, however, that the Irish have become more intense in their love for the island itself since they so seldom leave it.   A globe trotter would probably deny with indignation the statement that as his patriotism had broadened, it had become more shallow.   Nevertheless it is inevitable that a man whose native land, so far as he has experienced it, is bordered by his own horizon, must send his roots more deeply into the soil, than one who wanders for many years all over the globe.

The Irishman, so far as he has surrendered himself to the charm of the myths, the fables, the epics, and the legends of the early centuries, has become original in his literature and sentiments.   The flavor of his mind, we may say, has a finer tang, and a richer aroma.   Thus the Irish are more interesting.   When their lovable and ebullient natures are shot through with a knowledge of their delightful early literature, they become perhaps the most interesting people on earth.   They are as distinctive as Russians, but without that certain something which the Russians have, from which we of the West shrink.

The beautiful aspect of Ireland is best set off in the mind, very much as one painting in a room, accompanied by no other, gives that room a distinction and charm that would be marred by the addition of companion paintings. So the beauties of Ireland stand alone, characteristic, fascinating, ennobling. Just as a notable statue like the Venus of Milo was placed in a separate room, so Ireland, an island, distinct, without a peer, deep scarred by the glacier of history, richly dowered by lavish nature, is a picture in the sea having no counterpart. One does not compare it with other lands, because of its difference and its unique features. Thus those who like Ireland like it very much.

I was immensely interested to find an American of distinction, who had brought his wealth to crown his love for Ireland, and who had reassumed his ancestral castle and was carrying out the finer dreams of his ancestors, which they had been unable to embody. I also found in all parts of Ireland numerous persons who had returned from America, having acquired a competency. In not a few instances they have renovated the old homes and all about them are marks of thrift. We are familiar with this returning tide in Italy, but we have not thought of it so much in Ireland. Now that Ireland is ruled by the Irish, we may perhaps see an accelerated movement of this sort. One would say that only good can come from such a movement. The valuable features of the Irish character are too deeply ingrained to be lost by an American residence. On the other hand, the habits of enterprise and thrift, so outstanding as features of the American character, are often taken on by the Irish in America. They add what discouragement and lack of opportunity have often taken away from the Irish in Ireland.

The effect of increased resources upon the beauty of the Irish countryside may be very important. It may in time give to Ireland a finished appearance. The fields, even now, are not markedly different from those of England. They lack, perhaps, the intensive and general cultivation seen in England, but there is a quite general smoothness and evidence of continuous occupation and development. The cottages of Ireland lack the variety which we find in English cottages. The roof line of an Irish cottage is uniform, unbroken by dormer windows, and without the happy effect of an ell roof. It seems to have been a habit, if the dwelling were small, to add to it lengthwise rather than by an ell. Thus the beauty which the Irish cottage nevertheless possesses, is chiefly that pertaining to cosiness through the wealth of roses that cluster about it.

In another particular, the Irish cottages suffer by comparison with those of the more wealthy country. The surroundings are too often inadequate to the beauty of the cottage itself. Lack of leisure or of knowledge or stimulation has left the surroundings bare. The ancient habit of erecting the cottage close to the roadside, a habit common to all lands, has deprived it of any setting. Now and then an approach between hedge and walls is a refreshing feature, a prophecy of what all cottages may be like, when they are so situated. The general landscape in Ireland is far more conducive to charm as a cottage setting than the landscape of a level region.

Almost precisely the size of the state of Maine, Ireland is large enough to form an empire by itself. Compared with Greece or Holland it is large. There is perhaps as much fertile soil in Ireland as in the German empire.

Ireland gets its climate from America. In return it has sent a gulf stream of Irish immigrants. There are twice as many Irish in America as in Ireland, and of course, with their opportunities they have far more education and wealth. But they can hardly be better natured or more generous.

The climate of Ireland has contributed to its beauty. The generous rains accompanying the gulf stream clothe the island with continual green. Even the mountain tops, with rare exceptions, have verdure. The occasional bare rocky heights emphasize the fair fields below.

Even the peat bogs are sprinkled with myriads of bog cotton tassels, a flower always surprising by its white purity and delicacy.

The climate permits the growth of many forms not seen in America
[*Text continued on page 27.*]

FAIRIES IN THE HAWTHORNS

Irish lads and lassies know
Where the fairy hawthorns grow
For they've seen the little people
Nightly come and go.
A wee, tiny folk they are,
Flitting through the moonlight bars
In a fragrant rolling cloud
Of pink and white stars.
To the gleaming May-blooms
Come they in the gloaming,
Dandering and dancing
Down a little loaming.
With the homing bumble bees
Ride they on an elfin breeze
And from wings of butterflies
Flutter to the trees.
Curled beneath the broad petals
Deep among the boughs
Pipe they on their silver pipes
To birdlings a-drowse.
Long and long the fairies play
Over clouds of starry flowers,
Dancing with their feet entranced
By the moonlit hours,
Till the trumpet of a swan
And the curlew's call
Frighten them away at dawn
To a fairies' hall.
All the lads and lassies know
Where the fairy hawthorns grow!

Mildred Hobbs

THE VALLEY OF THE LEE

A HAWTHORN BRIDGE—COUNTY WICKLOW

HAWTHORN AND RIVER GRASS

SERPENT LAKE—DUNLOE P

AT SNEEM—COUNTY KERRY

MORE CASTLE—COUNTY COR

CARRIGANASS CASTLE—CO. CORK   A LODGE ROAD—CO. WATERFORD

IN COUNTY DOWN   IRISH ROSES—COUNTY CLARE

AUGER LAKE—PASS OF DUNLOE

TULLALEAGUE RIVER—COUNTY KERRY

north of the Carolinas. But the absence of our summer heats also permits such tree growths as we have in our northern states. Thus in the gardens calla lilies flourish, while the lime, oak, walnut, yew, beech and mountain ash grow to vast size.

The fuchsias grow to the second story windows, and appear in hedges in myriads in places eight or nine feet high. The foxglove runs riot, sometimes filling in entire roadsides. It has a habit also of peeping out between the interstices of the stones in old walls, and even cottages. Sometimes we saw it flourishing in a half dozen places through the old thatch, where, of course, it was most charming of all. The lupin, which at a distance cannot be distinguished from the larkspur, flourishes in great luxuriance. Stock and rocket grow like weeds. Even the potato fields are exquisite with pale lavender blossoms, which sometimes cover the plants completely.

The reader will not proceed far without noting that the author is no botanist, but happily that fact does not prohibit him from loving the beauties of Ireland.

ROSE COTTAGES

THE most distinctive feature of the homes of Ireland is the rose-bowered cottage. A great number of such cottages appear in this volume. There are parts of the Free State where every house for miles has rose decorations. Again, one comes to a region where nothing of the sort appears for miles. There seems to be no explanation other than the influence of example.

In many instances one finds a home, quite humble in other respects, but smothered with the rose and the honeysuckle, and even surrounded with gardens of roses. It may be that the interior of this cottage will have no floor, or only a rough flagging. It may be that those who inhabit it may not know a month in advance whether their living will be forthcoming.

The love of beauty is implanted in some souls and can be accounted for only by the goodness of God.

The most delightful feature is the mingling of the vegetable garden with the flowers. One will see rows of cabbages and onions, surrounded by a rose border.

The habit of whitewashing the cottages does indeed take away the mellow background which one desires to see. A farmer who had not whitewashed his dwelling would always apologize. Other improvements which would seem to be more necessary would not be mentioned. It is the ritual to whitewash the cottage, and even the garden fence. If the stone and mortar were allowed to show, the effect would be far more attractive. It has been found, however, that the roughly built stone bears the attack of the weather better when it is smoothly plastered, and even the whitewash fills some small chinks, and probably adds to the durability of the dwelling. One must deplore, however, the staring white, so common is this background.

THE COUNTIES OF IRELAND

IT IS a parlous venture to make choice of the most attractive county in Ireland. The choice depends on so many considerations. The almost purely rural counties have a charm indescribable. Cavan and Monaghan and Leitrim, small and inland, display rolling hills covered with fair fields, divided so numerously and so delightfully, and meeting the gaze at every rise of the road, that they win upon us till we forget every other consideration. Doubtless fertile fields, little farms, and snug cottages have an older appeal, and are rooted deeper in our ancestral loves than any other aspect of earth. I would rather look on a gently sloping, rich country-side than at any other natural object whatever. How much more dear and sweet it is than the cold majesty of bare mountains or the threatening ocean surges! How the little enclosures, bordering one another, with the low roofs between, each flanked by trees, each sending up its smoke, a signal of good cheer, take hold of every domestic and aesthetic sense and convince us of the idyllic perfection of a simple country life.

The sheep in the home meadow, the cows turning toward the gate, the generous stacks of corn and hay, the safe walls topped by hawthorn and, later, by the elder, but always with flowers below, the sense of peace, comfort, and sanity, all watched over by the distant spire, speak of the best on earth, and the care of Heaven. It was in this very country that Goldsmith wrote, and Moore. Here arose, while the Roman empire was dying, and before the days of feudalism, a society of simple saints like Patrick and Columba, who taught diligence, content, and kindness, and made a community rich in scholarship and poetry, while England was still almost savage. Search high and low, you will not find a fairer land, a better prospect, a kindlier people than in the better parts of Ireland. The love of such things is unforced; it is inevitable and eternal.

CONDITIONS OF TRAVEL

THE traveler has the choice of landing at Cork in the south, coming from America, or at Belfast and sometimes Londonderry in the north. From England there is a route from Fishguard to the south of Ireland, from either Holyhead or Liverpool to Dublin, and from Stranraer, Scotland, to Larne, near Belfast. There are various other routes from England and Scotland to Ireland.

There is a happy-go-lucky lack of information at Holyhead as to the transfer of motor cars. We were informed that no boats could go on the day of our arrival at Holyhead, and told to come back the next day, which we did, whereupon we were informed that the boat was full. We were from Friday until Tuesday attempting to sail. Everything seems to be done from London, but as motorists never hail from London, one requires to be at once an advance agent, a shipping clerk, a jockey, and several other sorts of person in order to start promptly from that port. We found conditions better at Larne.

At Dublin, on arriving, there is bad arrangement. One leaves the boat at Kingstown but the motor car goes on into Dublin, generally by another boat, and arrangements are very primitive here about unloading. One waits for the tide some hours. The customs regulations are being softened so that in future far less inconvenience will be experienced by intending visitors. It is of course for the interest of the Irish government to make it easier for motorists to enter the Free State. Entry into the Ulster government from Britain requires no such formalities.

When one crosses the line from South to North Ireland, if one is provided with a " triptych," it is the matter of a moment. One should exercise, however, great care in motoring along the border of the two governments, and keep on the main roads. Certain roads are not customs roads, and one may suffer very serious consequences by slipping out and in across the line. Those living near the line who are acquainted with the officials, and who are known to be crossing frequently for short distances may obtain temporary permits. It is better, however, for the tourist to do one of the states completely before going into the other, and so avoid a repetition of customs details.

In the small town there cannot, of course, be the same hotel accommodations as are expected in America, because there is so little travel, comparatively, in Ireland. In entering a town one should take note that the name " hotel " perhaps indicates only a place where liquors are served, although this is true of the British Isles in general. Americans will wish to go, of course, to the best place, and to the large towns or the resort districts. When we consider what Ireland has passed through, we should not be at all surprised at the lack of good accommodations everywhere. Very few of the hotels in Ireland are doing well. They are living in the hope that the present settled condition of affairs will induce larger patronage.

It makes little difference, in the arrangement of a tour, where the traveler goes first. He may, landing at Dublin, first swing south or north. The best course is to circle the coast one way or the other, making stops of some days, perhaps, at Dublin, Cork, the lakes, Galway, and the resorts in the northwestern counties, of which there are several of excellent character. The bugaboo of the west of Ireland is mere nonsense. It is the best of Ireland, whether for scenery or accommodations.

On our landing at Kingstown, my wife fell into conversation with a friendly civic guard, who said he took her for Irish because she had the perfect accent. This incident I am laying by for future disciplinary purposes. We were told by an English lady that she was afraid to visit Dublin, owing to Irish hostility. She thought it would be unsafe. Poor lady! the people of Dublin would not have known she was there, and if they had, would have paid no attention to her.

We were also told that we should be gouged on every hand and overcharged everywhere; that the hotels were miserable, the people insistent in their beggary; that we should be very careful of our motor-car and its contents. We found a better hotel in Dublin than any encountered in the provinces of England. We found a fine hotel in Cork, and some of the best hotels in the west of Ireland. The most dangerous individuals we met on the roads were a pair of beautiful colleens, one golden, one dark, walking arm in arm, so that we could not leave them without picturing them. With the exception of two wee waifs, nobody asked us for a penny, and one of these asked only for a ha'penny. We never locked our hotel rooms, and are none the poorer. The charges were all moderate and fair, and never in excess of those in England, and sometimes less for the same accommodations. We met only courtesy, though our inquiries were numerous.

The religious war, so called, was pleasingly refuted by the standing intact in the heart of Cork of a large, beautiful Presbyterian church of stone, and by the untouched condition of Protestant churches generally. Depredations and destruction there have been in plenty; but they were directed against those who opposed the freedom of Ireland, or who were believed to do so. I do not excuse it, nor even palliate it, but merely point to its cause.

One finds about the same sorts of road in all parts of the Free State. Many are good and most are fair, and none are without a stone foundation.

The thorough traveler may wish to cross through the interior of Ireland, which we did from west to east as well as from north to south. The finest scenery in Ireland, however, in a grand way, is more often found near the coast. The island has been likened to a saucer, with the high lands on the sea border. Nevertheless, there are not only many high lands, but some imposing mountain ranges in the interior.

The bogs of Ireland, which, one would gain an impression from reading, cover a great part of the state, especially the interior, are not nearly so extensive as we were led to believe, nor are they ever so extensive as to make monotonous traveling. The longest way through the largest of the bogs would require only a short run by motor. Most of them have been drained. One does not experience the sensation of dreariness nor vast extent when crossing the island in any direction.

The barest and boldest coasts are seen on the central part of the west of Ireland and northerly. In this region the mountains are frequently without foliage, but even here they do not constitute by any means the only aspect. There is now and then a district so rocky and broken as to prohibit agriculture. In the main the tillable soil is occupied and worked.

The greatest mistake the traveler in Ireland can make is to go rapidly. A hundred miles a day is always too much. The attractions of the streams, foliage, and the historical sites are sufficient to induce very many detours. An absolute getting ahead of thirty or forty miles, with detours of perhaps as many more miles, is all that should be expected.

HOPEFUL PROSPECTS FOR IRELAND

WE MET a fine old farmer who proudly said, " I am the best man of my years hereabouts." His home was cosy and neat. His speech sounded like that of a cultivated man. He was the soul of courtesy. His son, a man of middle age, brought forward a treat of strawberries, although we had stopped merely to get a picture of his home. A conversation ensuing brought out the fact that strawberries were sold at one dollar a pound in the neighboring market. The soil was perfectly adapted for producing these and other small fruits. It is one of many indications that farmers, if they become alert, may vary their one-crop methods to advantage, for no other farmer was similarly engaged.

At another point a housewife was complaining that her husband could find no work. Looking about, we saw fine fertile land, and asked if he could not raise all they required to eat, and if they had not plenty of potatoes planted. " No," said she, " there are so many weeds." That trait of mind, which can turn a man from one thing to another, and which has been called so marked a characteristic of the Yankee, might well be cultivated in Ireland. Those who cannot work for others, even though they habitually have done so, may often do something else.

DUNLOE

THE Gap of Dunloe is done under charge of guides who from of old have derived their living, somewhat precarious since the war, by taking parties through. There is no need of a guide. The way may be passed on springless carts. Horseback, as being more comfortable, is ordinarily chosen. It is perfectly feasible, at small outlay, to improve the road for automobiles. No doubt the hesitation in doing this has been caused by regret at taking away the living of the guides. But a toll road kept up by them might recompense them. This is the only place in Ireland where progress is stayed for such a reason.

Before the war one of the people of the pass used to fire a cannon and get fees for the echo. Powder not being available, he began to hello, which he still does. I told him my lungs were still good. It was pitiful to observe his hungry, hunted eyes looking for a fee for raising echoes. No doubt the resourceful chieftain who owns the domain, who was reared in America, and has bought in the ancient castle, will find a way more consonant with convenience and economics for the highlanders to earn their living. Another denizen of the pass blows a horn to wake the echoes, but complains that tourists are not responsive. I told him there were men in America who got a good living blowing their own horn.

The pass contains several small lakes, always pleasing among the mountains. Serpent Lake, where St. Patrick threw in the last snake in Ireland, is only fine in high water. Let us be glad he did a thorough job, for it is not the least among the pleasures of exploring the dark dells and rough deeps of Ireland, to be free from care lest one come upon a serpent. One feels a comfortable freedom everywhere. The kindly people and the glorious sky, the fair sweet country, help to invite our souls. Anybody can feel safe alone in Ireland.

Two little girls stood on a wall by the wayside on that bold and beautiful road from Kenmare to Glengariff. One held up a hand, as in school, and said, " Lift, please! " The request was so unusual that we heeded it. When they were aboard we proceeded to satisfy our curiosity. They had been eight miles from home, to confirmation, walking all the way. They had returned on foot two of these miles, and while not exhausted, confidently sought help in a manner as dignified and matter of course as could be. They lived just south of the long road tunnel. Our hearts were touched by their sweet simplicity, and we had a lesson in the perfect freedom and safety of these lonely mountain roads. They had no more fear than a child a block from home in America. When we thought of the children being carried to school in our land, and of the omission of school

ADARE ABBEY—COUNTY LIMERICK

THE TIME OF ROSES—COUNTY GALWAY

BY THE WHITE COTTAGE—COUNTY KERRY

UNDER THE GREAT BEECH—COUNTY KERRY

ROSS CASTLE—KILLARNEY LAKES

A DUNLOE COTTAGE—COUNTY KERRY

A CLIFDEN BRIDGE—COUNTY GALWAY

BENGOWER—COUNTY GALWAY

for a smart rain, the contrast was significant. The Irish became fiercely violent against old oppression, but were I alone on any road in Ireland, I should feel far safer than on any road in America.

The Gap of Dunloe passes by the sides of the highest mountains in Ireland. These mountains catch the ocean winds that accompany the Gulf Stream. We made this journey in a remarkably dry time. Ordinarily the mountains are an unfailing source of waters. Their rugged crests play with the storms, and the multiform shapes of the clouds are a continual delight. These mountains, the highest in the British Isles, are very impressive as seen from the ocean approaching on the west. They are unusual, also, in being nearly bare of verdure. Lying as they do between the ocean and the lakes of Killarney, they are a continuous challenge to our love of beauty and grandeur. In every aspect they make their appeal. In the terror of the storm they are magnificent, and one's spirit reaches out to delight in them. In the summer quiet they brood amid the cloud caps or the lower descending mists that clothe them. Seen from the lakes their broken reflections are an endless source of joy. They feed the souls of man as well as assuage his thirst. A region of similar beauty combined with grandeur exists nowhere else in Europe except in the Alps. The influence of the ocean is such that neither the cold nor the heat of Alpine valleys is felt amid the Irish mountains. They are wonderful at every season of the year.

The journey through the Gap of Dunloe and thence back to Killarney consists of a drive, a ride and a boat trip. The journey is the one thing that visitors to Ireland have got it into their heads must be done. We saw dainty ladies with almost paper thin soles pushing forward up the pass with an expression like that of the young hero of " Excelsior." The number of horses is limited, so that in days of large excursions it is impossible to take through all who wish to make the journey. One could read on the faces of the pedestrians a do-or-die expression, although there is nothing whatever difficult about the journey. It is not even steep, nor is it very long. It simply is not proper to make without stout shoes. It is, perhaps, true that this journey affords a greater variety, and confronts one more completely with notable physical aspects of Ireland, than any other. Yet one who makes this journey and no other in Ireland gets a very wrong impression of the island, which is green, soft, gentle and luxuriant for the most part.

The Laird of Dunloe, whose ruined castle, now being restored, stands at the beginning of the Gap, and who is a man of fine spirit and broad intelligence, is doing a great deal for this part of Ireland. Particularly he is supplying something which has never been plentiful there — funds to match the grand natural features with appropriate cultural features.

The river Laune, the outlet of the Killarney Lakes, is a short but exquisitely beautiful stream, and flows through the domain of the Castle of Dunloe. Here and there on its banks are luxuriant meadows and pastures and gentle slopes, all decorated with the magnificence of the Irish beech, oak, and lime. We hear much of the beauties of other rivers in Ireland, but we think there is more beauty in the short reach of this stream than can be found in a similar extent on any other river in Ireland.

PEAT

TURF, as the people call it, exists not on lowlands only, but often on the slopes of the mountains. An area of five hundred acres awaits, on the top of Bull Mountain, a suspended bucket line to bring it down. Peat is the poor man's fuel in the sense that it may be had for the labor of cutting and hauling. Five to ten shillings was mentioned as the cost of the right to obtain a year's supply. It requires about thirty tons for a family. Some farmers own their own sources of supply. The peat which dries nearly black is the best. When dry it is light in weight, and makes a pleasant fire, with smoke of a wholesome smell. It consists of solid vegetable fibers. It must dry in the open or it will heat and spoil. It should be protected from the weather when dry, but many families too poor to erect covering for it merely place the pieces on edge in stacks. Without a period of good weather for curing, great hardship is suffered. It is a poor fuel as compared with coal. But soft coal, at Killarney, for instance, costs seventy-five shillings a ton, a prohibitive price for the usual householder.

The cutting of peat and the drawing of it are among the more picturesque occupations of the Irish people. Formerly a young woman carrying a basket of peat was thought of as a typical Irish picture. The hardship involved and the time required for carrying peat by such a method would render its use impractical. The commoner way of drawing peat among the poorer districts is in donkey carts. The thrifty farmers have strong horses and large racks. In case a homestead is several miles away from a peat bog, the drawing of peat becomes the greatest of burdens on the household economy. If the source of supply is near, the fuel is obviously the best available.

Cutting peat is hard work. It is done now with a tool especially designed for the purpose. Two cutting edges come together at a right angle, so that as the cutting proceeds along a straight line, one thrust of the cutter frees a section of peat. Sometimes a whole family is seen at work procuring this fuel. One cuts and others toss out from the shallow pit the chunks cut off, while others stack them in such a manner that the air may get at every part.

The most usual vehicle met in the summer is the peat cart. A well kept up farm is noticeable for its huge peat stack, which in modern husbandry is housed under a stack roof. In the cabins, into the doors of which we looked, there was always, even in summer, a little fire simmering, so as to keep the tea hot. It should be understood that this tea is simmering or boiling all day long, and is the usual beverage. Infants are given tea so that by the time they are half grown they are as dependent upon it as upon their sleep.

The chimneys being low, and the door being for the most part open, the cottages are usually smoky. They are white without, but not within.

We have heard of instances of American stoves being set up in Irish cottages. We never saw anything but the ancient fire on the hearth. Of course it is not an economical method of heating, but the climate does not require any such scientific and careful provision against the cold as is found in America.

The use of peat through many generations has denuded a portion of the landscape of a great part of its beauty. In one instance we saw that all the turf around a dwelling had been cut away, leaving a rough, rocky surface in every direction. What the people of Ireland will do when the peat is exhausted does not yet appear, but we may hope that synthetic fuel will be developed. Fuel is in fact the greatest problem of modern times in all other lands also. Our civilization as at present developed is dependent upon fuel in plenty. If Ireland had such a fuel now, it might leap forward rapidly to a place of power and influence among nations.

THE PIG MARKET

IT WAS pig market day when we passed through Bandon. Big pigs were in their pride and the little pigs were making hogs of themselves as fast as possible. They capered, a noble six hundred, ahead of and behind us. They ran between the wheels and disputed passage with us foot by foot. They were very clean, and of handsome flesh color, outdoing all our imitations. There is much of interest in the pig kind, they are so full of uncertainty; one never knows which way they will jump.

The huge old porkers stood at bay, the litters of little fellows leaped about squealing. Others peeped between the racks of donkey carts. There was pig everywhere. But by slowness on our part, and a last leap on theirs, they all finally saved their bacon; but for good fun a pig market is no mean sport. Only, when they had all abandoned Bandon, and left not one squeal behind, one could have wished there were a better market place than the streets.

THE TURN BY THE STONE—GLENGARIFF

THE GAP OF DUNLOE—COUNTY KERRY

IRISH ARCHES—COUNTY CORK

MACROOM CASTLE

THE TOWN AT THE BRIDGE—LEIXLIP

THE HAUNT OF THE NYMPHS

LEIGHLIN BRIDGE—COUNTY CARLOW

AN IRISH HILL COTTAGE—COUNTY KERRY

BUNRATTY CASTLE—COUNTY LIMERICK

AN IRISH BROOK—GLANMIRE

AT OUGHTERARD—COUNTY GALWAY

A SHELTERED BROOK—GLENGARIFF

AT THE POET'S DOOR—COUNTY KERRY

A LOUGH GILL COTTAGE—COUNTY SLIGO

A RIVER IN THE FOREST

PRIMROSE COTTAGE—WESTPORT

The markets of country towns, in which list one must include all except the very largest cities, are an interesting survival of a custom which had its origin before history began. The names of some ancient Celtic and Saxon towns indicate that they grew up about markets. At first markets preceded shops, and everything was sold in the street. Even now the clothier, the shoemaker, and the faker may be seen spreading their wares for the day beside the fresh fish and the farming implements. Before early morning the lowing and bleating begin, and the buyers cast about discriminating glances. The bankers prepare for the day, and bargains are washed down with strong waters.

The wife and even the grandmother swarm the carts, and bring their produce. The roads at night are lined with farmers returning with their purchases. These are the great events of the year, for trade and for social greetings. Many persons see on market day all they are ever to see of the great world. The lasses get their idea of fashions, and tow home the swains they have roped. Altogether it is a wonderful occasion. He who has not seen a market day has not become acquainted with a country.

ILLUSIONS

THE Irish brogue is grotesquely overstated. The best English in the world is spoken in the great Irish cities of Dublin and Boston, in Dublin by the Irish, and in Boston by — others.

Coming to Scotland from Larne, in Ireland, I could hardly understand the speech of the shopkeepers, whereas at Larne and in Belfast I could with difficulty notice any variation from correct English. Only about one per cent. of the Irish speak Irish as their mother tongue, so I was told by a teacher of Irish. The variations from correct English in Ireland are slight in comparison with the North English dialect. The Irish have the gift of speech, and the English lack it, hence the Irishman can literally take the words out of an Englishman's mouth and better them. We have not forgotten that the Irish Burke was the golden orator of the House of Commons, and that Goldsmith and Swift were the brilliant literary lights of their time.

Those who understand and speak the Erse say that it is remarkable for delicate shades of meaning and for richness of vocabulary, supplying a word for every precise significance. It was brought to perfection by generations of scholars and writers who made of it a remarkable medium, — flexible, beautiful, poetic. And the present-day Irish scholars declare the best of the Erse compositions excel in literary merit the works of other languages.

To America, many years since, came the farm laborer of Ireland, who probably had less education than the rest of his countrymen, and less than he has now. The consequence was that we got in America the richest and most marked illustrations of the Irish brogue. A great surprise awaits travelers in Ireland when they learn that people with whom they converse usually speak as correctly as themselves, and often more so. A language which has seven words for water is not likely to lack liquid qualities!

It was long ago, to be sure, when Irish literature flourished, and it is a matter of opinion whether it will ever be revived to reach its ancient glories. We know what we think. But of one thing there can be no question, — the English-speaking Irishman usually has the Englishman and often the American at a disadvantage. He inherits a readiness and a range of speech. The Irish have long been known for their quickness of repartee, a thing which can happen only among people of quick wits and good vocabulary.

One of the consequences of the early richness of vocabulary is that the place names are significant and poetical. Volumes have been written by Joyce on this fascinating subject. The assumption of superiority by Americans who, from their supposed higher plane of knowledge, poke fun at the barbaric Irish place names, meets with a humiliating fall when the facts are once understood. For instance, the " bally," which begins so many Irish names, and which is seen in the English " bailiwick," merely means " town." The " kill," which often occurs in Irish names, is the ancient " cill " for " church." It has, therefore, the opposite from a gory significance. Similarly, the syllable " knock," in so many names, has nothing to do with the supposed Irish tendency to quarrel, but is the name for " hill." It is a curious fact that various names beginning with " O' " were of Norman origin in the portion of the name following the initial syllable. One might go on citing a thousand instances of similar character; but the writer is unfortunate in not being able to read, still less speak, the Irish tongue.

The dreamy, poetical, and highly appropriate place names of Ireland are a source of keen pleasure to one who takes the trouble to learn their significance. Thus another illusion about Ireland vanishes.

One meets in Ireland various repeated names, as also in England. The most notable instance in England is perhaps Avon, the Welsh, or rather Celtic, for river, which appears with great frequency. Similarly in Ireland it was natural that a syllable indicating something of the contour of the land, — like meadow, hill, stream, or mountain, — should enter into a great many place names. One cannot understand the history of Ireland with any thoroughness, without conning such volumes of place names. They are a deep mine of amusement as well as instruction. They indicate the customs, joys, troubles, and exploits of the ancient generations. We can, therefore, understand how persistently many of the Irish cling to the thought of the Irish speech.

As this subject is at the present moment in a vortex of controversy, one must be very careful not to stir up antagonisms. We only repeat some things that we have heard. One Irish farmer said that as six out of seven of the children of Ireland would emigrate, it seemed a pity that they should spend so much time in acquiring a difficult language, however rich that language is. Further, there is a very practical difficulty in that the teachers themselves, understanding Irish in very few instances, are obliged to take up, often at middle age, a new tongue — an almost im-

[*Text continued on page 59.*]

BONNY DALES OF IRELAND

In all the world no finer trees
Their heavy-hanging mantles wear;
No other meadows anywhere
Are covered with the green of these
Whose miles of vivid emerald spread,
Be-gemmed and flower-carpeted,
Through bonny dales of Ireland.

No other streams reflect the sky
From beds so jewelled and so green;
Their graceful velvet grasses lean
From braes of heather-bloom that lie
Like purple feathers quivering
Along the many streams that sing
Through bonny dales of Ireland.

And then the melody past words
Of dulcet music and sweet meaning
In the crooning and the keening
Of the waters, winds, and birds!
The music of the leaves astir
Where myriads of crickets chirr
Through bonny dales of Ireland!

The tinkle of the wether's bell
Among the flocks of snowy sheep;
The foaming falls where salmon leap;
And glens of woodland faerie spell!
In all the world there is no land
With spots more beautiful and grand
Than bonny dales of Ireland!

Mildred Hobbs

BONNY DALE—COUNTY DERRY

ROSE GATE—COUNTY DONEGAL

A BROOK SANCTUARY—COUNTY WATERFORD

A ROOF AND AN ARCH—COUNTY CORK

AMONG THE BEECHES—COUNTY CORK

possible task, and always impracticable. The Irish government is put to vast expense to carry out an ideal which, after all, is based on patriotism and romance rather than on necessary moral foundations. The genius of the Irish race will now reach a far richer and wider development by the use of the English tongue, because thus it may appeal to the wide world, and particularly to the vaster Irish population overseas.

If the Irish of Ireland are to continue to have fellowship with their brethren in Britain, America, Canada, and the other quarters to which the race emigrates, that fellowship will be fostered a thousand-fold more through the English tongue. We are not making any comparison between the two tongues. It is not necessary to heap obloquy or contempt upon either. However much one may mourn the going out of Irish in common speech, it seems almost inconceivable, judging the matter in perspective, that the Irish people in general can ever be brought to speak Irish. If they were to do so, it would hinder greatly certain currents of progress which we ought to try to foster. The Americans visiting Ireland are not helped by Irish road signs. If the use of an inscription is in being read, then the signs ought to be in English, because the tourists speak that tongue.

The undoubted and unchallenged continuance of Ireland as an independent government has now done away with one of the principal reasons for reviving the Irish language. We of America are not in any danger of losing any aspect of our nationality through our use of the English speech. No more are the Irish in Ireland. Just as certain Hollanders, especially a notable present day novelist, wrote largely in English to secure a wider public, so also the Irish, exercising their brilliant talents in a linguistic way, should be able in their literature to appeal to the entire Irish race, which they certainly cannot do if they limit their literature to the Irish language. The genius of the Irishman seeks to extend its influence in the world at large, and the trend of the ages is the breaking down of speech barriers. We may almost say that the influence of the

Irish race in future depends upon their not only understanding, but speaking the English tongue, whatever other languages they may know.

An extreme sensitiveness is voiced in the Irish Parliament on the matter of the Irish language. The government has at times been accused of laxity in pushing the teaching of Irish in the schools. We do not know of any other nation which insists on teaching two languages in its elementary schools; yet Ireland does this. It attempts to go contrary to what has been found practical in the world at large.

It is of the highest importance that pupils who develop a taste for languages should be thoroughly trained in the Irish tongue, especially those children whose families speak it. Such persons, carrying on their knowledge of the language to such an extent that they may be able to use it in a literary way, and interpret its past masterpieces to the present generation, will be of great value to the state. They will keep unbroken the historical continuity of Irish thought, and will set forth for us the romance of the past. They will preserve the legends, myths, and epics of the other ages.

In short, the great advantage of the Irish tongue will be its masterly knowledge by a few, who shall impart its thought to us, rather than a weak and beggarly smattering of the tongue among millions, who, from their residence and occupation, or their other limitations, cannot go far enough in the language to enjoy it or to derive any real benefit from it.

In concluding this chapter on illusions, it is well worth while to say anything possible to overcome the prevalent notion that the Irish are naturally a quarrelsome people. That they are tremendous fighters when aroused, no one, they least of all, will deny. That they have furnished for many generations a great part of the armies of the British Empire is also obvious. We may, however, explain that fact in part by the meagerness of their home opportunities. When the ancient Irish land tenure obtained, there was little hope for an Irishman who did not leave his country. Their youths easily listened to the siren voices of the recruiting officer, and the debt of England to Ireland for a large portion of its fighting forces is so great as to overbalance, probably, any sacrifices that the English have made for the Irish. But it would certainly seem that months spent in Ireland by the writer would have shown some indication, somewhere, of a quarrelsome spirit, if indeed it is inherent in the Irish character.

We sometimes forget that the Irishman has been the under dog politically for a thousand years, more or less. He has felt hostile to government, because, up to a recent period, the government was against him. The habits of thirty generations cannot be broken in a moment. It may be that the writer does not at all understand the Irish character, but so far as his observation goes, he has never seen a quieter country, a more accommodating people, a people more ready to smile and to make the best of a bad situation. Undoubtedly, entrenching upon what the Irishman considers his rights would rouse him. We do not, however, find much bitterness against the English. We think it is a great error to attribute the outbreaks of a few years ago to Irish quarrelsomeness.

It may excite astonishment or laughter that the writer should maintain such a surprising thesis as this is, that the Irish are not quarrelsome. I feel certain, however, that no small part of the reputation of the Irish for quarrelsomeness arises out of the peculiar conditions under which they have lived. We think the comparison between the Irish and the Italian character in this regard will show that not one Irishman is in a broil, where many Italians are. The writer wandered through the streets of Irish towns many evenings, and never saw any discord, nor indeed heard any. The funny columns are to blame for giving a wrong impression. They have given a totally wrong impression of the Yankee farmer. They have kept at this so persistently that the average city dweller thinks of the rural inhabitant as a " hick." The consequences are that city people, particularly those from the great cities, when they go into the country, experience a sudden awakening.

Similarly the Irishman was the butt of a generation ago, in American newspaper jokes. He was set down as of the quarrelsome type. In some cities, where the Irish predominated, the hoodlum, being an Irishman, was supposed to typify the Irish character. But every race has its city gangs. The Parisians are notorious in this respect, and what nation is not cursed by this element? The Irishman in America, accumulating a little property, and having a home of his own, is as agreeable to deal with as a man of any other nationality. It is universally admitted by those who know the Irish at all, that they have most sunny dispositions. They are able to make the best of a bad situation. Had this not been true, they would long since have perished from the face of the earth. They can extract fun from the dreariest subjects, so as almost to get bread from a stone. Is there any-where a people more ready to accommodate, more generous, more loyal in friendship? I have friends among the Irish on whom I would depend to any extent, in the greatest crises of life. This is true in spite of a difference in religion.

I should be far from maintaining that the Irish are perfect. There are national vices, just as there are national virtues. We do, however, find less surliness in the Irish than is observable in many other nationalities. We find in them a disposition to make the best of a bad matter. Particu-larly they are responsive to higher appeals, patriotic, religious, or social. They love their friends as faithfully as they do their own families. In the cultivation of these fine natural characteristics are found the best hopes of Ireland. If the Irish in Ireland have not seemed to exhibit general busi-ness sagacity, the same cannot be said of them in America.

The conclusion is inevitable that the difference in conditions is respon-sible for the difference in development of character. While business sagacity and frugality are not the highest virtues, they make possible some virtues higher than themselves, and they lay the foundation of a complex and beautiful civilization. The happy-go-lucky character attributed to the Irish in Ireland may, for the reasons we have set forth, be supplanted gradually by a more steady and hopeful push in education and in material conditions.

SOCIAL AND ECONOMIC

A MERICAN money is a large influence in Ireland. It comes with persons who buy their homes and lands where their fathers dwelt. The climate, the scenery and the love of romance and a real philanthropy is influencing such men as the laird of Dunloe. Then the American tourist spends, and if the department of intelligence is well managed, the tourist in Ireland should increase a hundred fold. The most usual source of American money is, however, that sent over by friends or relatives. Its effect depends on the character of the persons who receive it. On some it has a pernicious effect; to others it is a veritable godsend.

In general through Ireland, the six out of seven in a family of children who go to America will of necessity have a dominating influence on the thoughts of their parents, and on the development of Ireland. We were much interested to find not a few persons who had returned to Ireland, having accumulated a competency in America. Here in their ancient land they are merchants or comfortable farmers, and are spreading the economic ideas which they learned in America. They have better agricultural machinery and are doing things in a way which helps to lead the whole Irish life into more thrifty channels. There seems to have been little attention given to this reflex tide of emigration from America to Ireland. Probably the fuller tide westward obscures attention to the smaller number of returning emigrants. But one who returns has with him a hundred times as much, in the way of money and purpose to develop the country, as one who goes out. In process of time this returning flow is likely to have a very powerful influence in the island.

The American money that is sent to Ireland to relatives and friends is of course used in part to assist them to leave Ireland. In other cases it helps them to complete the payments for their lands, under the Purchase Act now in operation. The American money that goes to Ireland through the expenditure of tourists is of course a most profitable revenue. Tour-

ing in Ireland is becoming increasingly pleasing, owing to the interest which
the Irish themselves feel in the country. Tenants who have bought their
farms and are now, therefore, landholders, feel a more vital and permanent interest than those who are awaiting an opportunity to get away.
The Irish feel now that they have hope of developing their land for
themselves, rather than for landlords. Even in the case of landlords,
the modern demand for better homes is so insistent and universal and
appeals so strongly to our sense of what is due to human dignity, that there
are many instances in Ireland of better housing where land in still in the
hands of landlords.

An obviously heroic effort is being made by the Irish to render Ireland
more accessible. Serious economic growths, however, never have important
development based on sentiment alone. The natural attractions of the
country and the effort to meet tourists half way must of course govern the
volume of tourist traffic. This book itself is intended to make it apparent
to the hesitant and the doubting that there was never a better time to visit
Ireland. Its natural beauties are eternal. Peace reigns in the land. Americans are everywhere received with greatest heartiness. The people of
Ireland believe in our ideas, our ideals, and our coinage, as they have
every proper reason for doing. As Switzerland lives mostly through its
tourists, the development of Ireland is likely to proceed largely through
the same source. It is no disparagement of Ireland to say this. The
country is a sufficient call to the world, if only the Irish do their part.
The wealth that was in Ireland was driven out to a great extent at the
time of the transition of government, through the unwarranted but perhaps
natural fear that the change might bring instability. That influence has
now probably passed its climax, and the turn of the tide has begun. It is
not likely that the English will return in large numbers to Ireland. The
inspiration and means for Irish development must for many years come
from America. This is not to say that Ireland lacks numerous enterprising
and forward-looking men. If, however, those men have not the accumulated interests behind them, it is impossible for them to carry forward

Irish development. English money for Irish investments is not easily had at present. The hope that German money invested in power schemes on the Shannon or elsewhere will eventuate in any great benefit to Ireland is, to say the least, doubtful. If Ireland is to be saved, it must be by the Irish. Backed by such moral and financial aid as their American friends can give them, they will not be without the necessary enterprise. It is as well to admit at once that enterprise has been almost a minus factor in Ireland for many years, owing to the pernicious system of land tenure. The sense of hopelessness and the uselessness of human effort had become pretty thoroughly ingrained among the poorer people of Ireland.

It may require one, it may require ten generations before this spirit of apathy passes away. In case, however, an Irish farmer has bought his land, a change so far as he is concerned may be rapid and hopeful. He knows now that so far as he improves his acres, the improvement redounds to himself.

Urban development will take care of itself. It has never anywhere lagged behind rural development. Always, in every age, that side of a country which has needed watching economically has been the rural side. Combinations of farmers to assist one another in obtaining machinery and such other credits as are necessary, will be formed. An American traveling in Ireland, who is looking at the country with a practical eye, will form the judgment that the greatest need is to extend man power by machinery. Practically everything is done in the ancient way, by hand power. Here and there new methods have established themselves. It is easy to see that such extensive crops as are raised by modern farming methods in America may be obtained in Ireland. The natural richness of the soil and the advantage of abundant rain, and the intensive method fostered by the nearness of Ireland to the best world markets should produce far better results than any we have attained in America. Combinations such as are seen here and there in the development of creameries bid fair, in time, to change the face of the country. Better conditions of living, by the improvement of the homes, and more regular and profitable methods of employment, will bring about great results.

One can but notice a squinting expression on the faces of many, possibly the majority of the aged cottagers. It arises from the smoke of their cabins and from their darkness. Large windows and better cooking facilities, and better drainage, will establish the health and increase the sense of dignity of the people. All great reforms come slowly, but they come. It is not an argument against this statement to allege that conditions in Ireland have always been practically what they are, and that therefore they will never change. After all, it is fair to admit that Irish agriculture has been handicapped for many years to a greater extent than that of any other country. The success of the Irish in America may serve as a prophecy of what will come in Ireland. It is quite unfair to say that since the Irish seem to be content with mean conditions, they always will be content. The change in France after the Revolution was rapid, although it was retarded by the terrible toll which Napoleon took of its manhood. Despite emigration, there are still people enough in Ireland to make the country as wonderful in an economic sense as it is now in an esthetic sense.

The farms of Ireland are mostly small, and happily so. On many not even a cow is kept. But don't feel distressed for the poor people of Ireland. There are a couple of goats on the farm, and one good goat is better than a poor Kerry cow any day in the week. We met a farmer at Lismore who had many broad acres. A goat followed him about on the banks of the canal where I was at work. This interesting animal tried in vain to eat the brass thumb-screws on my tripod, and finding they were securely fastened, then twisted up her horns in the tripod legs. This was too much, and we extricated her with some difficulty. No wonder that a goat with an appetite so omnivorous should give four quarts of milk a day! The goat may not be beautiful, but a hungry child thinks otherwise. The goat's udder is very large. If a cow's were as large in proportion, she would give a barrel of milk. Further, children grow fat on goats' milk, and the goat gets its own living.

GATE OF THE GIANTS' CAUSEWAY—COUNTY ANTRIM

A SHELTERED BRIDGE

THE LAUNE AT DUNLOE—COUNTY KERRY

MOTHER'S COTTAGE—COUNTY DOWN

PARADISE REGAINED—COUNTY WICKLOW

THE BRIDAL OF THE BEECH—COUNTY CORK

A MIDSUMMER DREAM—COUNTY SLIGO

BY THE ANCIENT RIVER—COUNTY CORK

One often sees these beasts fastened together. In fact, if you present a nice new clothes-line to an Irish housewife, she immediately cuts it up to make goats' tethers, and persists in going any distance, even to the other side of the farm, to hang her wash on the thorn bushes, where it never blows away. This sounds humorous, but it is no joke, in the sense that it is absolutely true. These goats, thus tied together, as the motor car approaches and the road is narrow, huddle at the side, and prepare to jump over a wall. Dick says that they count three to time their jumping. But Dick is a lawyer, or on the way to be.

The goat, being a great wanderer, is as likely to be found at the top of the highest mountain in Ireland at night, as by the back door, unless some means be found to restrain his roving disposition. It seems pitiful to tether the goats so that they have to hop out of the way, timing fore and hind legs in perfect synchronism. Still, the reason why a goat exists is to feed where nothing else can be allowed free. But what the poor people the world over would do without goats is a puzzle to say. Feeding here and there, without care and without preparation for their living, they bring the farmer a larger income on his investment than any other possible beast.

Once let these animals get free, and they make for the hills, which they love. There are wild goats in the Irish mountains that have thus escaped the old homestead, and seem not anxious to return. There is no way of capturing them except by shooting.

Of course, the pig is common enough in Ireland, but he is not, as some humorous papers have tried to teach us, omnipresent. In fact, some farmers seem not to enjoy the raising of pigs. But poultry is universal, and people who seldom taste fresh meat otherwise, eat their own poultry.

INTERESTING CUSTOMS

WHEN you approach an Irish cottage, the housewife, or the farmer
if he is at home, immediately comes to the street. The cottagers
are so in the habit of giving directions, and seem so to enjoy it, that it is
doubtful if they would welcome the introduction of more sign posts.

It is a part of the ritual, if you call at an Irish cottage, to have a chair
placed in the garden for the guest. The necessity for economy in a small
house is such that it is taken for granted that the visitor will not care to
go indoors. I was much interested to see how ingrained this custom had
become, when a dear old grandmother brought her best chair, and placed
it in the center of the garden, although it was raining in torrents. She
had connected the idea of a caller with placing the chair, and was most
probably somewhat flustered.

As we would prepare to make pictures of cottages, the housewife would
run for her scissors to cut off the roses. We were obliged to restrain her,
because we wished to have the roses in the form in which they grew. The
housewife would fill our car with roses at every cottage, if we allowed it.
When we declined this favor, they would say, " At least, let us bring you
a drink of milk." This would occur before the poorest cottage. The
hearts of these people are naturally most kind.

Near Sligo we came upon a farmer whose premises bore every mark of
prosperity. As we slowed down, he came running behind us to see what
was wanted. Our admiration for his place of course met with a ready
response. He had large plats of vegetables surrounded by borders of
flowers before his house. In a second enclosure, outside the rows of vegetables, against the walls there were ranges of beehives, and between each
pair of hives were blossoming shrubs. The bees had only to step next door
for a load of honey. This was a delightful conceit, which was new to us,
but the decorative feature taken as a whole, the blossoming vegetables,
flanked by the beehives and flowers, was one of the most pleasing sights

imaginable. This farmer delighted in his home and in his country, and had even made a quatrain on the delights of Ireland and her homesteads. The thatched cottage, he averred, was not only the most beautiful in the world, but the warmest in winter and the coolest in summer. This man was a philosopher; he recognized that Ireland had not attained all that she desired in a political way, but he was of the opinion that it was best to take what could be had and to make as much of it as possible.

It is obvious that in every country men are slow to commend their own calling. It may be partly from reticence and pride. It is, however, often because they know the drawbacks attending their particular kind of work, whereas they do not understand the drawbacks connected with other walks of life. It is therefore cheering to hear men commend their own calling. We think we found more satisfaction among the farmers of Ireland than we should find among those of America. The majority of farmers everywhere find existence not easy, and a good homestead with modern improvements is nearly impossible in most cases, if these improvements are to be paid for from the farm proceeds. When, therefore, we found, as we did in a number of cases in Ireland, men who had extended their premises and enlarged their fields, and were obviously getting ahead and believed in their work, it was an excellent sign for the future.

CONTRASTED BEAUTIES OF IRELAND

THE most marked feature of Irish scenery is the contrast between lake and mountain. In this sense we should properly use the word lough, which is the same as the Scotch loch, and with the same meaning. That is to say, it is not confined to fresh water, but refers to any enclosed, or nearly enclosed, body of water, like a lake or bay. Ireland abounds in certain parts with lakes, but the entire shore, which runs into thousands of miles, if one follows the contour, is a kind of multiplied Mount Desert. With almost no exception, the entire coast of Ireland may be said to be bold. In not a few instances the islands rise like mountains in the sea, and suggest the Greek archipelagoes, except that the Irish islands are covered with foliage, where there is any opportunity for growth.

The ride along the Sound between Achill Island and the mainland reveals a scene of striking beauty, as narrow as a river and superior to the Hudson in its most attractive course. The winding of the road, now near the shore, and now skirting the crests of the cliffs, opens every moment a new outlook. The stone cottages, the numerous walls, the hay stacks, the feeding herds, the play of the shadows across the mountains and the Sound, or in different moods the resting of cloud caps over the loftier peaks, provide a series of pictures, changing in a quiet, slow, majestic motion. The varying surfaces of the salt sounds of Ireland, sometimes covered with white caps, sometimes absolutely smooth, but best of all with little touches of wrinkled water here and there, breaking the reflections into bands, supply us with materials for beauty so abundant that our whole mood is one of joy in the wealth of the world.

These scenes belong to all who will take them, and they refute the pessimism that presumes we must pay for what we get. The beauty of Ireland is not lost upon its own people, proving that the statements we have just made are true. Possibly the people who live on a charming shore have never sought to express categorically their sentiments regarding it. Very few can do that successfully, and I do not belong to that select number. But I know that charm may exist without the possibility of analysis.

One of the finest effects of the salt loughs of Ireland consists of the coloring of the cliffs by the tides. At low water there is seen a series of bands, beginning with the green of the lower seaweed, and changing to a lighter green, then to brick reds and iridescent greens, and a half dozen other shades mysteriously left upon the rocks, by the influence of the tides on the chemicals in the rocks. In that long and marvelous stretch of mountain and lough seen on the southern shore, as one goes westward from Kenmare, there is exhibited a variety of contour and color difficult to duplicate in beauty elsewhere in our beautiful world. Rocks break through

THE VALE OF OVOCA — COUNTY WATERFORD

RHODODENDRON STREAM — COUNTY CORK

THE POOL AT THE FALL — COUNTY CORK

A FLOWERING ROOF — NEAR BRAY

BELOW ST. MARY'S — TRIM

BETWEEN YOUTH AND AGE — COUNTY MEATH

THE OLD AND THE NEW — TRIM

ST. DOOLAGH—COUNTY DUBLIN

TOWERS AT SWORDS—COUNTY DUBLIN

KILLARNEY ROSES—COUNTY KERRY

A HAWTHORN STREAM—COUNTY CORK

DERRY BRACKEN

BLACK HEAD—COUNTY CLARE

DUNMORE—COUNTY DOWN

the surface of the loughs, little peninsulas reach out here and there, each with its bay differing from all others. The endless forms of humble sea life, clustering on the rocks or on the seaweed, add their quota to the general theme. There are a score of miles, yes, even thirty miles of this marvelous coast. At times, on a clear day, one looks off to the other side of the lough and the opposite peninsula that reaches seaward. The mountains rise on that side also. Here and there winding paths or narrow roads make off into the lower hills. Beautifully arched bridges span an occasional narrow reach of water, so that one has the elements of beauty on both sides of him.

Some of the coasts of Ireland, on a raw day, exhibit a magnificence that is fairly described as awful. The tremendous cliffs of Antrim and Donegal and Clare are so lofty, and the roar of the waves breaking at their base is so like a cannonade, that as one faces the power of the wind it almost disputes standing room, and the effect is one of magnificence and terror.

It is said that if all men were distinguished, none would be so. Ireland suffers from the number of its beauties. As we stand on some great rock boulder breasting the sea, we think our position is one of singular attraction. The next day, or the next hour, even, we may pass to another headland and in its various appeals forget the wonder of the headland that is passed. It is probably impossible to find elsewhere such a succession of various beauties combined with grandeur, as one sees on the Irish coast. The boldness of the Pacific coast of America, while very striking, lacks the attraction of the numerous inlets found on the Irish coast, where harbors are plentiful. The three great fleets of Britain have made their rendezvous at Bantry Bay, with room to spare. The attractions of Queenstown and Kingstown harbors have been descanted upon by every traveler, especially by those whose leisure allowed no further exploration of Irish scenes. No one has overstated the attractions of these two remarkable harbors. But most of the estuaries on the Irish coast still remain to be celebrated by the hand of a genius. The poet Moore did much, but he left much to be done.

After all has been said concerning the difficulties of travel in Ireland, it is probably true that one can travel in the island today with more comfort than at any previous time.   The slowness and dust and crowds incident to coaching were such that only very vigorous or determined explorers saw the remote coasts of Ireland.   Thackeray believed himself to be a good deal of a traveler when he had made his journey, yet one may today not only follow his track, but reach many points which to him seemed inaccessible or too remote, and that without danger or difficulty.   Indeed, the modern motor-car has made it possible to see Ireland with greater ease and greater thoroughness than ever before.   We confidently await bards and novelists who shall do fuller justice to the so far unsung glories of remoter Ireland.

The erosion of the waves, acting on rocks of different degrees of hardness, has produced on various parts of the shore, and particularly in Antrim and Donegal, so called natural bridges.   To an imaginative mind, especially in the heroic and mystical period of history, it was easy to believe that these bridges were the work of fairies.   Sometimes they were assigned to less respectable artificers.   The devil comes in for an undue share of attributions in Ireland, as elsewhere.   Anything particularly awful or remarkable is as likely as not to be attributed to him.   It is a sad commentary upon the cast of the human mind, which we hope the appeals of scientific habits may change.

Inevitably, solitary and bold coast cliffs, especially when detached from the land, as at Carrick-a-Rede and elsewhere, were an irresistible invitation to the lords of old days.   They fortified such points, and the ruins of their old towers are a feature in Irish landscapes.   They remind us of the age of the country and set in train our imaginative musings.   Thousands of such cliffs or fortified heights in the interior bear names indicative of the former use to which they were put.   Expressive and appropriate designations acquired by such fortified heights give them a charm admirably fitted to stimulate the artist and the romancer.

ARCHITECTURE OF IRELAND

MY ATTENTION was given more particularly to such aspects of the architecture of Ireland as lent themselves to pictorial uses. The subject of Irish architecture, however, is fascinating and somewhat remote from the trend of the architect's studies, in the sense that he may never have investigated the simpler forms of architecture in Ireland, since he has had the rich features of English and French Gothic within convenient reach.

There still remain in the northwest counties some examples of the bee-hive cottages. They resemble very closely the Eskimo *igloo*, except that they are somewhat more pointed. They are without question the earliest form of dwelling place to be used in a country where timber is not plentiful. It has been noticed that many of the seventeenth-century dwellings, even in America, had very low doors. It has been forgotten that doors were intended not merely to make ingress possible for the owner, but difficult for the enemy. Thus we find that the beehive cottages have doors so low that it is necessary to stoop or even creep through them. It is a sure indication that their inhabitants wished to be able to defend themselves, which they could more easily do with small doors, against which they could roll great stones.

Some seventeenth-century dwellings were of very handsome style, like one the author owned, whose door was so low that the average man would hit his head on the lintel. Other arguments have been made from this circumstance to prove that men of the middle ages were smaller than modern men. I think a far more reasonable inference is that the doors were made small for the sake of defense. However this may be, when the more substantial modern stone cottages of Ireland came to be erected, their doors and their windows were small. The doors were often Dutch; that is, they open in halves, one above the other. This was convenient both in Holland and elsewhere to keep out strolling animals. In fact, more than once we saw a donkey or a horse standing by a door with his neck well inside, looking over the lower portion.

The cottages are marked with the peculiarity that they extend in one line to indefinite length according to the needs of the growing family, and the enterprise of the owner. Almost never is there a wing or an ell, and we noticed no farm cottage in Ireland with a dormer window. Further, strangely enough, there is seldom a gable window, and often no window in the end of a cottage. Even if there is such a window now, the chances are that it is not original. This is one of the puzzles of Irish architecture, because the loft was a convenient place to sleep, and in other countries we find it always used. The attics of Ireland are generally dark, or open without floors.

The effect of continuing the cottage in a straight line of course detracts from its cosiness of appearance, but in some cases the length is so great as to be humorous. In not a few instances we noticed that where the contour of the land was slightly sloping, the cottage followed that contour. Hence it was a real sidehill cottage.

Although these drawbacks prevent our considering the Irish cottage as anything other than the simplest possible form of square house, it is still true that as a background for flowers the cottages may become beautiful. Any building which has not positive faults is beautiful in the proper environment. There is nothing in the style of an Irish cottage which offends. Further, its walls are often of a very substantial character. In the earliest time, and even now, the walls may have been put together roughly with rubble and mud, or they may be of well-fitted stone. It is, however, much to the credit of the Irish people that as a rule they have sought to build of stone. In this connection the early ecclesiastical architecture is said to be largely wattle and daub. The statement is probably true enough of the smaller edifices, but for the larger churches there is no reason to suppose there was not a substantial character given to the walls by squaring the stone, at least roughly. Even in some of the small dwellings and churches we find carefully-trimmed stone.

BRIDE'S NEST—COUNTY WICKLOW

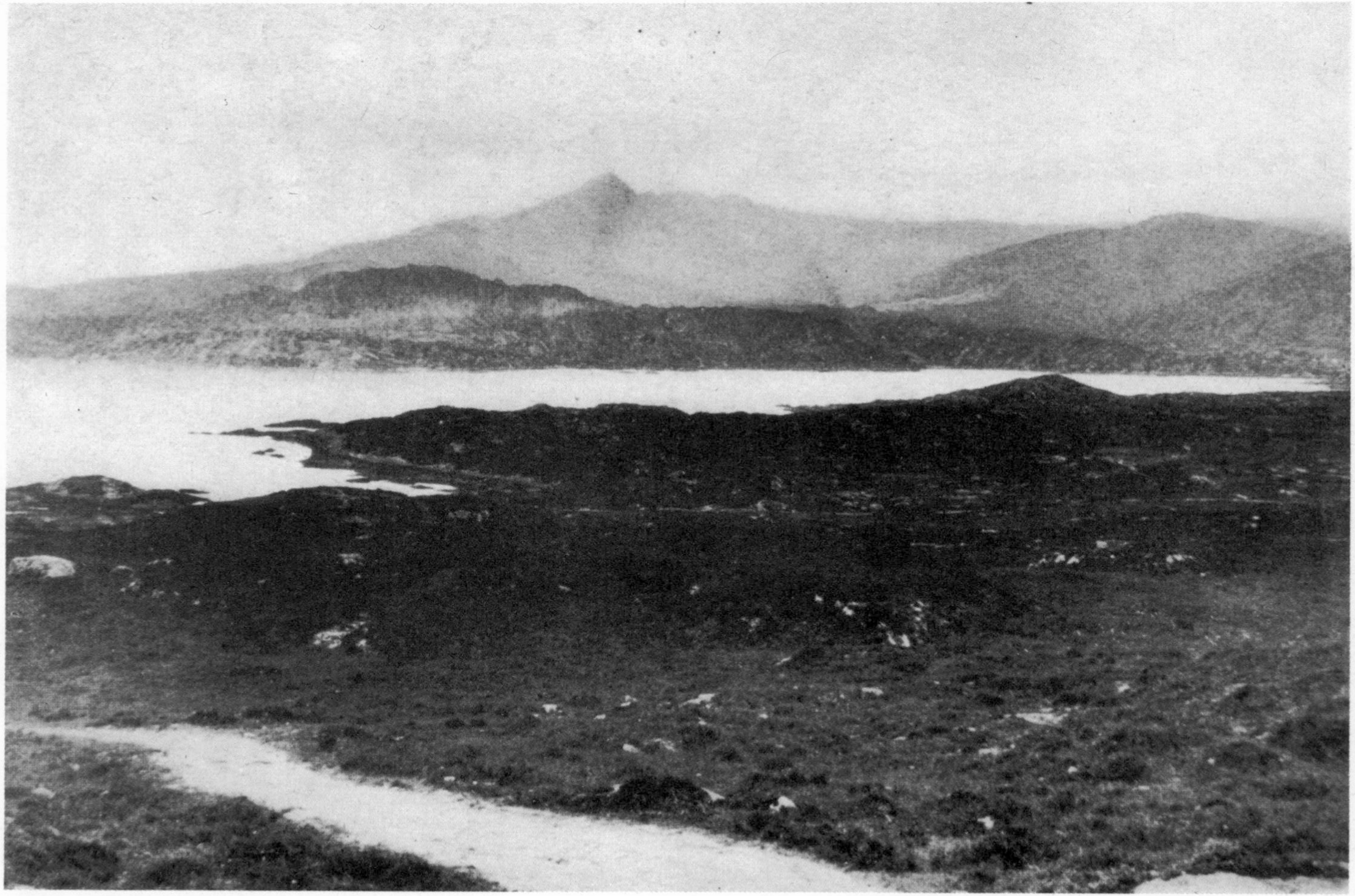

BANTRY BAY—COUNTY CORK

ON THE QUOILE—COUNTY DOWN

DEEP DALE—COUNTY CAVAN

The particular in which the later Irish cottage differs from the earlier is in the chimney. We have lost sight of the fact that the chimney is really a modern matter. Before Queen Elizabeth's day chimneys were rare. Not a few Irish cottages, some of which are pictured in this book, show no flue at all on the exterior, but only an opening where the thatch is plaited, and through which the smoke escapes. One would say on first thought that such a dwelling would be consumed at once by fire. Experience has shown that some such cottages have endured for hundreds of years, and that they very seldom catch fire. In fact, in my entire tour of Ireland, I recollect seeing only two or three cottages wrecked by burning. Of course, a smoke vent of this sort is a primitive carrying forward of the circular hut. The opening itself was a concession to improvement. Whereas in most cases a chimney exists, we observed in a few cottages that the chimney top merely came flush with the peak of the roof. The chimneys are almost always short, and seldom rise more than a couple of feet above the roof. They are therefore far more picturesque in this respect than English chimneys, which, to secure a draft, are often carried to a considerable height and give the effect of instability. The floor of the Irish cottage, being of earth or flagstone, is ordinarily on the same level with the hearth. The peat fire does not draw well, owing to the lack of air beneath the peat. This difficulty is overcome in one cottage I visited by the ingenious application of a smith's bellows, in which the air is driven by an enclosed rotary fan at the side of the fireplace, and a tube is carried to the center of the fireplace opening below the peat. The hugeness of these fireplaces creates the impression that they are really the end of the house, as they nearly fill it. Of course they are never filled with the fire, nor is that the intention. The housewife works about the fire on either side, but within the fireplace. The spacious effect of the one-room cottage is out of all proportion to the small size of the edifice. When, as is often the case, the entire interior is one room, a pleasing breadth and depth are obtained. The walls, containing all the utensils of the household, and the dresser appearing with its plenishing, and the settle bed next it, give an effect like that so much sought in modern camps. One feels that all the household property is in sight, and the inhabitant is in the midst of his belongings. A sense of plenty is created even when it does not exist.

It is well that the cottager can make the most of what he has. Both the settle and dresser are shaped always in quaint, and very often in excellent lines, and in many instances they are carved. Their owners do not seem yet to be aware that they possess in their heirlooms a very large intrinsic value, which could be used in case of emergency to carry them over a period of famine. In a cottage with two little square windows we found sets of solid interior shutters, which were built with blocked panels in the shape of a Greek cross. These panels were precisely like those used on the seventeenth-century oak chests, both in the British Isles and in America. The particular set of which we speak were attached with quaint and dainty hinges, original and complete.

A serious objection to the present structure of the Irish cottage is, of course, the meagerness of the windows, which we see is being overcome here and there by their enlargement. The greatest handicap under which the cottages suffer is the lack of a cellar. The climate of Ireland is such that owing to the usually depressed location of the cottage, the floor is often damp, and not seldom the water oozes from the floor. As a consequence pulmonary troubles are common. Of course, the making of a cellar would greatly enlarge the cost of a cottage, since the foundation walls do not of necessity go far below the ground, according to the present construction. The frosts do not require deep foundations. The health and progress of the Irish people, however, will compel the erection of a more modern style with a cellar. This cellar will not be wholly an additional expense, because it may serve for storage and to this extent will obviate the necessity for erecting another building for that purpose.

There are two ordinary methods of covering the roofs; perhaps we should say three. The simplest method in the old time was to use thatch. This will last about ten years in fine condition, and after that, by patching, for perhaps five years more. It is a common practice to add new thatch to old until in some instances we measured the depth of three feet! Such a depth adds greatly to the picturesqueness of a dwelling, and incidentally the width of the projection at the eaves really constitutes a covered porch, three or four feet wide, on either side of the house. At the present time the thatch costs as much as a more permanent construction in slate or tile, in case it is necessary to hire the work done. Those fortunate and adaptable farmers who have caught the knack of thatching, and can therefore mend their own roofs, are likely to continue the use of this roof, which stands for so much in our literature and in our thought of the old days. As, however, the thatch can be mended only in dry weather, and there is not too much dry weather, the cottager finds it difficult to improve his roof without neglecting something else. The thatch straw, rye or sometimes of wheat, must be carefully prepared and sorted to secure the best results.

A slate roof, of the heavy native slate, is no less attractive to the eye than the thatch. The heavier and the larger the slate, the more pleasing is the effect. I personally measured slabs two feet across, and where a lap of three thicknesses occurred on the roof, we found sometimes six inches of stone! Where the wall is also left plain, the effect is amazing. One would suppose the cottages grew from the ground, and had stood forever. In fact, if the work is well done, such a cottage is almost eternal, because the timber sustaining the roof will never rot. The modern slated roof is most unpleasing, nor is it even so durable as the heavy old slates.

The method of tiling roofs so common in England and in some sections of Ireland gives a rich, mellow aspect which, contrasted with the brilliant surrounding green, is effective. We do not, however, often find a marked iridescence in the tiling, and a tile roof may therefore be said to be the least picturesque of the three coverings.

Where slate is laid, numerous species of moss attach themselves at the intersections of the stone, producing an effect so fascinating that one lingers long in delight. The coloring of the moss varies through all shades of yellow and green. It grows in patches. Its mottled coloring, a random effect of nature, exceeds in charm anything that could be planned by man.

Even in case of the thatch, when it is neglected, mosses sometimes form upon it, and in particular the foxglove roots itself on the roofs. On one cottage we observed a half dozen sturdy stalks in full bloom! The saddle of the roof is sometimes covered with sod, where the grass grows luxuriantly, and blends gently on either side with the thatch. We could never tire of these various roof effects. They in themselves are enough to give distinction to the humblest cottage.

It is a part of the ritual in Ireland, as in Wales, to whitewash the cottage, and even the garden wall. In many instances, where the interior is rather black, the cottagers would apologize that they had not done their spring whitewashing on the exterior. It seemed useless to expostulate and say that the natural stone was far more attractive and less harsh than the brilliant white. Where a rough wall is plastered, probably whitewash assists in the preservation of the wall. We could not, however, resist the feeling that whitewash should be applied within rather than without.

It may seem humorous to consider a straw stack a work of architecture, but when we remember the etymology of architecture, and see the elaborate forms of thatch on some of the better cottages, and stacks, we must revise our views. The stacks, in conjunction with the cottages, double the charm of the homestead. Everywhere in Ireland we saw the coming in of that modern horror, corrugated iron, for the roofs of the dwellings, and for the open pavilions where straw is stacked. A few years of improvement in this direction will ruin the beauty of Irish rural scenery. Of course where labor is of much value, the age of iron must make itself dominant. We would like to believe, however, that it is an intermediate stage on the way to roofs of stone.

The porch of an Irish cottage is usually non-existent. Semi-occasionally we find a small stone porch coming to a peak. The surroundings of the Irish cottages are sometimes all that could be desired. There are charming instances of hedges at the sides of the flagged approach. Many cottages have a row of rose bushes ranged against the wall, and a few feet from the wall another row, making a walk between. Not enough is

made of the gable ends of cottages, where the variation of the outline
forms a perfect background for decoration. All that will come in time.
As the old cottages often follow the shore lines, they are, from the water,
beautiful beyond description, especially as night draws on and the smoke
of the evening fires is seen rising here, then there, and at length proceeding
from every chimney on the long sweep of a sickle shore. A cottage fire
means so much, and is so suggestive of the return of the farmer, of the
welcoming children, of the evening meal, of the rest at evening, that we
feel its symbolism is richer than any other rural element.

Barns are not a large feature of the Irish life. The mildness of the
climate is such that merely a shed or shelter is sufficient for the animals.
This is one more instance of the influence of climate on architecture. A
soft and mellow air like that of Ireland inevitably induces a certain simplicity of architecture. Free from the necessity of fighting against the
bitter blasts, the people find it is feasible to carry out certain effects in
building which would be impossible in a cool climate, where the architecture must be more severe and less attractive.

The earliest church edifices in Ireland engage our interest, not only
from their architecture but from the great names of good men who are asso-
ciated with them. The most astonishing relic of the old day is to be found
in the roof of a dwelling or two and a church or two; the old church
edifice on the rock at Cashel, and the House of St. Columba are instances,
as well as is the roof of St. Doolagh, near Dublin. If a man ever attempted
to worship the work of his hands, he would be assisted in his veneration by
these wonderful roofs. They are very pointed, pitching at an angle of
about eighty degrees, and are formed of solid stone carefully cut with the
beveled surface conforming to the roof, and, of course, braced within to
prevent their falling in. It is probable that the pitch is so extreme, that
these roofs might stand without such bracing. They are the earliest
thought of man in the attempt to obtain a pointed arch. It is perfectly
obvious that the method of those false arches of Mycenae was identical
with the construction here, insofar as the laying of the stones in horizontal

sections is concerned. Presumably, in a bitter climate, these roofs might not stand, but their fine condition, after so many centuries of weathering, indicates that in Ireland they are feasible as a permanent method of construction. That these roofs should be rare is not strange, because Ireland, never rich, could not afford the accurate cutting of stone necessary in this sort of construction. Where they do appear, they stand out as marvelous monuments of the simplest but most effective sort. It is true that an architect bred in a school of design which demands an adequate and logical basis for an arch for carrying anything that is not perpendicular, may challenge the shape of these roofs. It is also true that such roofs would not be feasible on a grand scale. In the Milan Cathedral, where the roof is very flat, so that one may walk about on it, it is necessary to construct great interior arches to sustain a vast superimposed weight, and it is also required that stone should be cut with a projecting lip so that each may shed water onto the next lower. But in small edifices like those we are considering in Ireland, time has shown the stability of the method of construction, which does not require anything like the massive supports within such as would be necessary with a lower pitched roof. There is also a unity of effect in the wall which seems to proceed from the perpendicular walls to the roof without changing style, and gives an effect of permanence and a sense of natural growth from the ground itself.

This rare construction was probably rather difficult, as well as beyond the means of the builders, but we may rejoice that we have a few examples that rival in their interesting features the best works of the Greeks before the classic period. When we travel in Ireland the general effect of the church architecture upon the stranger is surprising. He finds that in the majority of instances the good church edifice of a town belongs to the Protestants. This arises from the long dominance of Protestant power, and the fact that a great deal of wealth was in the hands of the Protestants. The Irish church, officially corresponding to the Church of England, is represented very generally, where Protestants are found, by churches that suggest the English village church. In great cities the Catholic church has naturally made an effort to erect edifices worthy of the numbers attached to that faith. Particularly at Armagh, is the vast and noble pile on a very strategic hill, and with an approach perhaps unparalleled and certainly unsurpassed, the Catholic church has erected a cathedral at the center of its historic diocesan scheme. As the central authority of all Ireland, the Archbishop of Armagh has now this dignified and appropriate seat. Doubtless it represents the love and devotion of millions.

In Dublin, and in Cork also, and various other cities, Catholic cathedrals of dignity and fair proportions have arisen. I noted in particular, in the small city of Tuam, an edifice which represents a great deal of local energy and sacrifice, being as it is of dimensions and style far beyond what one would look for in a city of the size of Tuam.

I cheerfully take this opportunity to enter a protest against what I consider to be an unwarranted criticism of the Catholics of Ireland. I have heard it said on more than one occasion that the splendid and inspiring architecture of the church edifices contrasted too greatly with the humility and poverty of the cottages, inasmuch as it was from the contributions of the cottagers that the churches arose. My impressions are directly contrary to this criticism. When the age of Ireland is considered, and the various reflexes of prosperity which must at times have blessed it, I certainly could not think that the people have been impoverished to erect the churches. Before the disestablishment of the Irish Church, — that is, the Protestant Episcopal Church of Ireland, — of course the general taxation went to support the Protestant church, just as now obtains in relation to the Church of England. We of America, even when we are Protestants, cannot come to see the justice of such taxation. But without desiring to stir up any spirit of rancor or controversy, plain justice and decency would lead one to point out that those who criticize the richness of Irish churches in contrast to the comparative poverty of the land, have evidently overlooked the fact that a vast number of those churches are Protestant, and that directly or indirectly they have been paid for in proportion to their means by the Catholic people, through forced contributions.

It is natural that in a reaction from this condition of things, the Catholics should exert themselves to the utmost to obtain at least certain noble edifices at their centers of population, or historical worship. The parish church of Catholic Ireland is not so good as one would expect it to be. But when one has scanned all the facts set down here, it is quite obvious why the Catholic church is a simple edifice. These circumstances impressed the writer more than any other one fact in his Irish pilgrimage. For long distances the Catholic population must still walk to church. I have elsewhere referred to finding two girls who walked eight miles each way for confirmation. That was not an instance of overchurching. It is true the district was a mountainous one. But in general, in a fertile country, there are certainly no more churches than are needed by the devout population.

Our conclusion, in relation to churches in Ireland, is, therefore, that the greater part of the fine edifices are Protestant, but built by taxation in part of the Catholics; that the few great Irish ecclesiastical edifices are largely recently built as a free offering by the people, and that the parish churches in general are rather simple and far apart.

By far the most distinctive ecclesiastical edifices of Ireland, however, are the monastic establishments. As in Britain, they existed in large numbers, and at some of them the population, monastic and lay, connected with the central establishment, numbered several thousands, as at Cong. It was at such establishments that the Irish language reached its fullest literary development, and the torch of culture rose with splendid effulgence and lighted great parts of Britain and the Continent. At such establishments pupils were received from various parts of Britain and of the Continent, and the letters of such men as Anselm to their loved preceptors indicate a refinement of manners and a versatility of learning equal to that enjoyed in any age. The great missionaries of the church, about the period of the sixth century, went from Ireland. Kings delighted to honor the friars of monasteries, and not seldom would they lay aside their regal robes to assume the humble garb of monks. The monasteries and nunneries became retreats for persons of culture and wealth as well as for the lowly.

CATHEDRAL AT DOWNPATRICK

THE LIFFEY FALLS—EUSTACE

A GLENGARIFF BRIDGE—COUNTY CORK

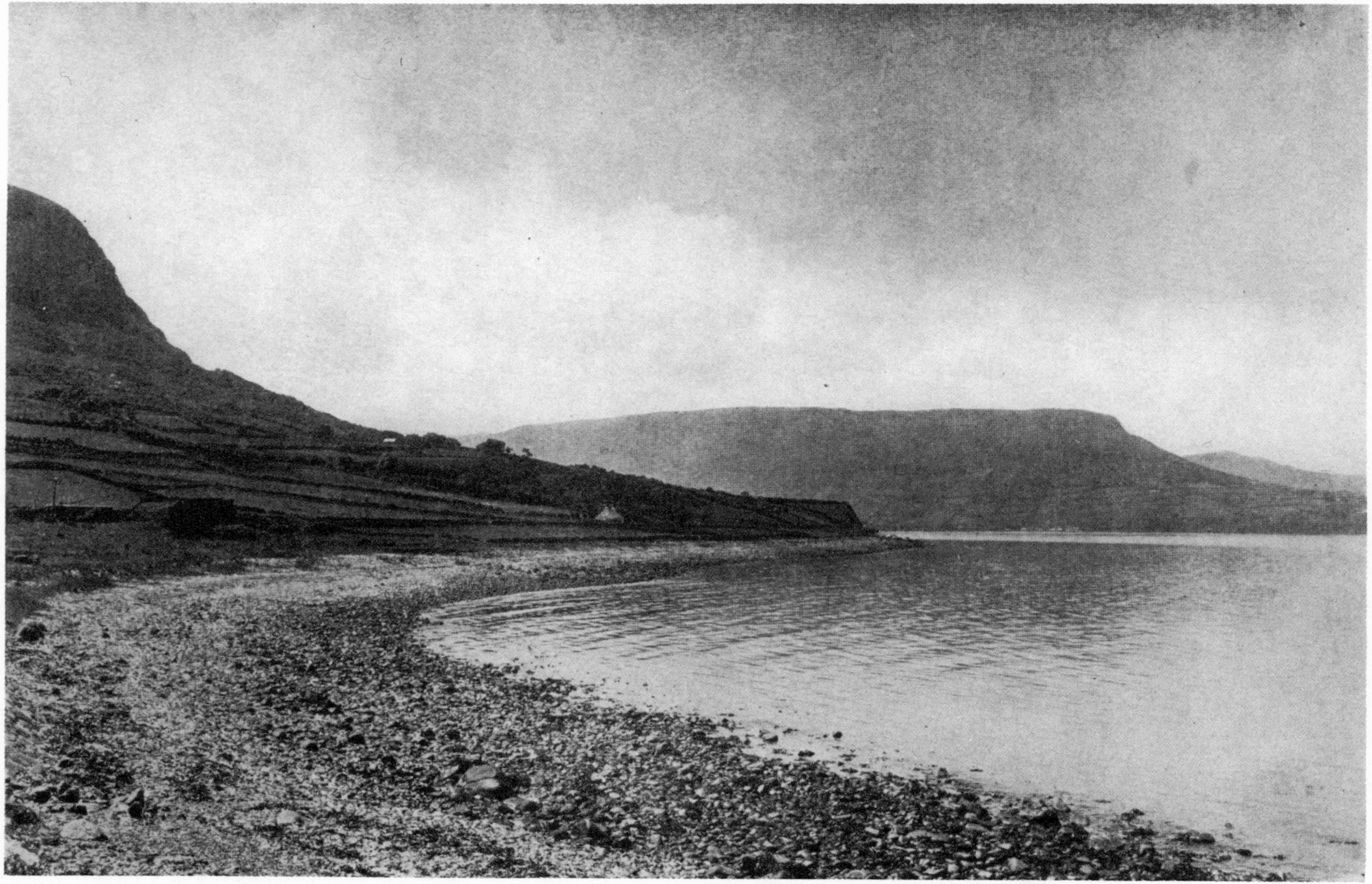

THE IRISH COAST—COUNTY ANTRIM

Such great establishments were often fortified, and, according to the custom of the day, the abbot exercised a commanding influence in political matters, or was even a lord in the feudal system. The economic organization of a great monastery, a thing quite strange and apart from our modern knowledge, is one of the most fascinating studies of antiquity. There was a head to every part of the organization. Wide lands were cultivated. Some gave themselves to culture of the earth, and others, who had a genius for books, either commented upon the pages of the ancients, or wrote in golden and silvern letters on scrolls of purple, the sayings of the saints and sages.

There is not so much variety in the monastic establishments as one might look for. The usual type had a somewhat slender, square, lofty central tower with a spire. The chapel windows were generally traced in the Gothic fashion, with some degree of elaboration. The dormitory windows were simpler, but of durable style.

Everyone who goes to Ireland knows of the picturesque charm of Muckross Abbey. Here and on various other sites the cloister garth was the picturesque center of the establishment. Some noble trees — a yew, a walnut, or an oak — often stood at the precise center of the garth, and sometimes reached such height and spread as to overshadow it entirely, forming an agreeable shade in summer; while in the case of the deciduous trees, the pale winter sunlight was admitted through the bare branches. In this respect, those who eschewed the yew tree had the advantage. The yew, however, was often chosen for its immense and almost eternal vitality. The yew does not know when to die. Doubtless the passion for eternity, which is hidden in the heart of every man and particularly appealed to the monks, induced them to decorate with the yew. We find it, therefore, not only in the garth, but about the various church yards and in castle gardens. The color of its bark and the intensity of its dark shade form together one of the most beautiful and striking aspects, of a decorative sort, about the ecclesiastical edifices of Ireland.

In instances where, as at Adare, an abbey stands in the open fields, it affords the modern man the most perfect object of romance, of reverence and a love of the permanent and the old, that has come down to us. Of course there are instances in Ireland, as in England, of the secularization of abbeys, which, at the time of their sequestration, were given over to favorites or persons whom the monarch of the period felt must be repaid for services in war. In other cases, abbeys are inextricably mingled in town dwellings in such a manner that it would require an antiquary and a detective to see where the walls of the sacred edifice ended and the dwelling houses began.

We do not find the richness of sculpture that was usual in France, or even in England. There are notable exceptions, however, which will be noted in detail. We need to recall to mind that the abbey was not built primarily as a work of art, but as a residence for its brotherhood. It was a common home, with its chapel, its refectory, its dormitories, its cloister, its kitchens and offices, — a term used in the British Isles so much, and so little understood in America. If the culture or the accumulated wealth of an abbey or the benevolence of the political power were favorable, the abbey might develop into a noble, perpetual example of faith. Otherwise it remained merely a residence of the monks.

One finds that at every age of the world some particular flair of the human mind has led itself into extremes in some peculiarity of architecture. This age doubtless will be marveled at centuries hence for its thoroughly unreasonable skyscrapers. The feudal age carried to an extreme its castle building. The monastic age tended very strongly to concentrate at the monastery the architectural work which at a later time would more naturally be scattered about the entire face of the country. In towns of France everything is concentrated upon the cathedral. So in Ireland, the monastic establishments were very numerous, and seemed to gather to themselves nearly all the civilization of the country. There is perhaps no place on earth so conducive to the poetical and historic imagination as an old abbey. Wandering about its environs, or winding through its old passages, it is easy for one to glide into the spirit of its life, and to re-people it as it was a thousand years ago. It is in such surroundings that Tennyson loved to be. The historian in such a situation should be able to infuse some warmth and color into otherwise dry pages. As we stand by the ancient tombs and scan the mute effigies of those who were once loved as leaders in the world outside, or in the abbey itself, as we note the noble spring of the arches in the chapel, and follow again the ghostly steps of the monks about the ambulatory, as we see the little cells where they rested and prayed, we are impressed by the fact that the monastic establishments were the connecting link between the imperial period of Rome and our modern times. They preserved as in amber some of the best thoughts of men which would otherwise have been lost. It has been well said that men laugh where they should weep, and weep where they should laugh. The saddest matter for contemplation by an intellectual man is the loss of human thoughts, that were germinative and stimulating. We are occasionally imagining that in these days we know nearly all that is worth knowing, but as lost arts are lost, we can form no estimate of their number or importance. The genius of man, in reacting upon those who possessed it, may have developed their spirits into glorious personalities going on somewhere now. But for us, when we rummage the treasure chambers of the past, we are often shocked by being confronted with crypts of bones, the inanimate skeletons of thought. What would have happened to the world without the preservation and renewing of ancient thought through the monasteries, we do not know, but we do know that the world would have been infinitely poorer. Even so, where scholarship and taste were lacking, the monks sometimes destroyed ancient treasures, erasing a literature of spirit and of power and writing over it humdrum palimpsests. We cannot forget that perhaps the most valuable of Biblical codices, dating well back into the fifth century, was discovered in a monastery on the sides of Mount Sinai. Modern times have been largely engaged in reassembling the thoughts of ancient times. There is no commoner thing in the world than the delusion that we are original. The writer or speaker who prides himself on having forged out a bright and burning thought is a thousand times to one merely restating what somebody else has said better, one or two or three thousand years before.

In one particular the American is shocked in going about Europe, to find that the authorities who care for the ancient churches or monasteries are so familiar with delving among the dead that they have lost a proper respect for the sad remains of our mortality. The guides point with gusto to the storehouses filled with human skulls, very much as if they were bins of grain or objects of legitimate curiosity. Is there not enough of the kind and covering earth at least to conceal what is left of vanished men? Must we be jostled about like footballs? One can but feel that it would be far better taste to inter the pitiful relics of our race. Particularly one sees everywhere about Europe that graves are practically rented, and on short lease at that. In some of the most respectable districts in England and Ireland, the skeletons of the ancient fathers are ruthlessly tossed out to make room for the children. Indeed, there is no feature so humbling, or even so insulting to our poor humanity, as the careless method of relinquishing it to a fortuitous future. Far better the cleansing process of devouring fire, which was common among the ancient Irish, than this contemptuous treatment of bodies which once may have housed noble souls.

The living have for many centuries desired to be placed at last to rest beneath the droppings of the sanctuary. Certain spots have been supposed to be especially sacred. While, of course, we believe that the earth is all the Lord's, yet this eager preference for a particular place of sepulture is responsible for that jostling in graveyards, so common about old foundations. In the very interior of the edifices we walk over the dead. We are glad to believe that God is too great to confine his benedictions to particular spots, and that the effluence of his life is to be found everywhere, so that the martyrs in the forest are equally at home with those who are enshrined under the sacred altars of the abbeys.

The castle building of Ireland is another and ancient aspect of architecture. Probably the castle of Dunluce, on the North Antrim coast, is the most celebrated, and justly so, of any in Ireland, owing to its marvelously picturesque location. It satisfied all our preconceptions, formed in child-

ELOW THE ARCH—CO. KERRY   OWENGLIN BRIDGE—CO. GALWAY

ANTRIM CASTLE   ADARE ABBEY—CO. LIMERICK

A BROKEN STREAM — COUNTY CORK

THE BRIDGE COTTAGE—COUNTY WESTMEATH

ARCHES—COUNTY KERRY

A HILLSIDE FARM—COUNTY KERRY

THE BROW OF THE HILL—COUNTY CORK

A PETALED MEADOW—COUNTY CORK

A KENMARE CASCADE—COUNTY KERRY

KERRY COTTAGES—MILLTOWN

TULLAGH CHURCH—CO. DUBLIN   THE HILL OF SLANE

OMAGH—COUNTY TYRONE   KILDARE TOWERS

hood, of a stronghold. Standing on a rock, almost detached from the shore, and looking out to the wild strength of the North Atlantic, its strength and extent and history are enough to stir the imagination of a pale ghost. Probably Ireland had as many castles as any country in the world, for the reason that at an early time there were so many chieftains, and the wealth of all was so entirely in cattle that their guard and defence were the principal businesses of life. A similar condition existed in Scotland, especially on the border. In Ireland almost every castle was on the border, in the sense that at some period it was necessary to defend it from a too near neighbor who was not neighborly. Numerous square towers of moderate extent occur throughout Ireland. Into the ground story were driven the cattle, at night, while the family lived above. We find somewhat similar conditions in portions of Italy, and doubtless in other lands.

A castle was the usual guard of a ford where in later times a bridge was erected. The castellan exacted a toll, which went under the name of protection in the case of all who wished to cross that ford. Thus Athlone in its name and location suggests the origin of its castle. It was perhaps the most important of the castellated fords. The other castles were erected merely from the strength of their natural positions. Others guarded the estuaries of rivers, while still others protected the passes in the mountains, like the Castle of Dunloe. We find Ross Castle, on the lower lake of Killarney, dominating the lake, over which it was able to send its swift police boats. Thus it was a dull chieftain who could not find a place or an excuse for the erection of a castle. No one can complain that they fell short of their impulses in this direction.

In process of time the liege men of a chieftain naturally had their huts about his castle, and in this manner all the earliest towns grew up. At Waterford, Dublin, and many other points castles were erected to protect particularly good harbors. The marauding Danes, or the enthusiastic pirates of whatever name, who descended upon the Irish coast and made good their footings, at once rehabilitated or erected a castle.

In the interior of the country, also, even where there was neither river, nor pass, nor hill, the lord of the land felt all the more need of the castle wall. Thus in the open country we are met with extensive remains of great strongholds, like More Castle. While the romantic appeal of these grim old fortresses reaches most modern men, and has great influence over the writer, it would seem that when the half-formed purpose of many a man, to restore a castle as a modern residence, comes to the point of final action, too many objections arise. For some reason men find it more agreeable to erect an entirely new structure rather than to make use of the old. For one thing, the absence or paucity of windows in castle construction is an objection, and an almost insuperable objection, to their restoration, unless one is to spend more upon the old than a new edifice would cost. But such expenditure has not prevented the restoration of old dwellings. So strong is the desire for connecting the past with the present, and so great is the pleasure of the fine reaction incidental to dwelling within a comforting stone wall, that in process of time a good many of the ancient structures that are not too far dilapidated will be availed of to form ideal homes. People carry from great distances sculptured stones to incorporate in modern dwellings. Why not leave the stones where they stand, and add such features in the way of restoration as are necessary?

It is true that the castles of Ireland passed through a siege recently almost as grievous as the battering of Cromwell. During the transition between the governments, an element of the people who were out of hand made rough work with many of the old castles. We found one instance of a ruin for which an award of more than eighty thousand pounds had been made toward restoration, which award in the shuffling of governments was reduced to a sum of less than one fourth of that amount. As a consequence the owner will not rebuild, and the people about will not have the benefit of employment in restoration. As one inspects the various ruins of Ireland, one sees that the work of Cromwell was lamentably thorough in that scarcely a castle ruin remains which does not bear the marks of his attack.

After we have considered all these causes of decay, it is probably true that the vast majority of castle ruins arise from the differing trend of the modern age, which leads men's thoughts elsewhere. Formerly the strong men dwelt in the castle. Now the castle dweller is more likely to be the dreamer, the poet, or the inheritor of an age and a spirit that has passed away.

Nevertheless we are indebted to the Irish castles in no small degree for the charm of Irish landscapes. Washed by the river's flood, or crowning the crest of some old cliff, covered with mantling ivy, they give the last necessary touch of charm to a landscape redolent with natural beauty. We have found by extensive experience that while the public visit castles, they seldom enjoy pictures of them. Castles are better in the background of lives or pictures than as prominent features. In their place, as reminders of struggles and purposes of past ages, they will remain. We saw but one new castle in Ireland, and even that had an ancient nucleus. It is doubtless a proper sentiment, which is induced from the trend of our century, to leave the castles to molder. Anyway, their stones are mostly monuments of tyranny. It is seldom that a castle has escaped connection with some event the author of which wishes, if he is still where he may wish, had never occurred. A castle belongs to tyranny, and while the manner of its destruction may have been as tyrannical, that destruction nevertheless is a part of the trend of the age. This volume might be filled several times over with the picturesque ruins of ancient feudalism. We have shown a sufficient number of them to indicate their place in the history of Ireland.

The bridges of Ireland are a prominent feature of its architecture. They are more impressive, perhaps, than all other features combined. Their structure is almost uniformly of stone arches, and some of them are old enough to have lost their history. We were highly amused at one lady who told us of a Roman bridge built in the year 1400! It is quite the habit in England, and sometimes in Ireland, if a bridge is very old, to refer to it as a Roman bridge. Of course there are some Roman bridges in England. The nicety of construction in Roman bridges, by which the stones are consolidated into one mass by the marvelous Roman cement, easily distinguishes them in England from modern work. In Ireland, just

west of Glengariff and in many other places on the old disused roads, there
are small bridges with a flat and delicately crested arch, which have doubtless stood for some centuries, but we very much doubt whether there are
stone bridges remaining from the classical times of Ireland. In those days
the ford was usual. In a region not troubled by floating ice, the ford was
more feasible than in a colder climate. The so-called camel's back bridge
is not infrequent in Ireland, although the spring of the arch is not so sharp
as we find it in Spain, for instance. Nevertheless, it is sufficiently picturesque to win our admiration. The railings of the bridges were mostly low,
and of course of stone, but with no special effort at ornamentation. The
bridge was a wholly utilitarian structure. Its beauty is incidental to the
arch necessary for solid construction. The pointed buttresses of the arches
on the upstream side, like the prows of boats, are no small feature of the
beauty of bridges. When, as often, ivy or other vines cover the structure
in whole or in part, and a stream of broken water flows beneath, and a
stone cottage or old castle stands at one end of the bridge, one's feeling for
composition is fully satisfied. The most quaint and pleasing of the bridges
not only rises but narrows toward the center. Its contour from an airplane
is still more pleasing than from the ground. For the most part, if the bridge
is seen at a slight angle to the river, it shows more fine proportions and contributes to the composition with a greater satisfaction than when it is seen
from any other point.

Though heavy rains, sometimes continuous for many hours, fall in
Ireland, the bridges do not seem to have suffered from destructive floods.
The instances to the contrary are so rare as to be almost negligible. When
bridges are made with a water table like the Clifden bridge on page 38,
this little touch of architectural design adds to the grace of the structure.

Fortified bridges in Ireland, as elsewhere, are extremely rare. The
Clifden bridge is provided with a watch tower, but whether of very ancient
construction we doubt.

Stone walls do not, perhaps, properly belong in the architectural class,
but they provide us with the most interesting feature of the Irish landscape,

A VALE OF KERRY

STEPS ACROSS—COUNTY CORK

THE ARCHING ASH—COUNTY GALWAY

A HARMLESS IRISH SERPENT—COUNTY KERRY

A KILLARNEY DRIVE—COUNTY KERRY

INVER BAY

A FISHERMAN'S BRIDGE—COUNTY CORK

aside from the green fields and the trees. In one of our pictures we show no fewer than twenty-two ranges of stone walls, one succeeding another. When fields are thus broken up into small sections, the effect is peculiarly pleasing, though perhaps not fully definable. It gives a sense of neighborliness and fellowship, because one feels that there has been coöperation, and the unpleasant effect of landlordism, of which one is conscious in a vast field, is escaped. But there are a great number of finished walls, about estates, terminating in gateways, of wonderful charm. We have featured some of these.

From infancy the writer has been fascinated by gateways. Their immense variety of design gives no end of scope for architectural genius. Further, the gate itself stands for mystery, and human curiosity is aroused to wish to know what lies beyond it. An open gate is the finest embodied form of invitation which it is possible for man to construct. There was a time when gates were important. The gate-keeper's lodge was as much a feature of a gentleman's place as the residence itself. In a few instances Americans seeking to reproduce European conditions have erected gate lodges. Of course, in actual life, the gate is either left open or the gate-keeper is not in evidence. We can understand the natural desire for privacy when weary men return to their homes. In an age when the boor is in the saddle — that is to say, the owner of an automobile, — he pushes in where gentlemen fear to go.

The solid walls which line so many roads in Ireland are in their season a feature of wonderful charm owing to the fact that they are often topped by turf, on which grow the daintiest little daisies in great profusion, and this of their own initiative. In fact, even where no turf is placed on a wall, flowers will thrive, apparently on a few grains of sand. The effect of a road bordered on both sides by a volunteer array of daisies produces one of the most beautiful effects imaginable, which will live in my memory as long as anything in Ireland. How these hardy little flowers can live and bloom in a dry time is past understanding. For weeks together no rain fell in Ireland, but the rich, full border of daisies continues apparently without suffering, almost as hardy as everlastings. Up and down hill these borders go, and even across the bridge rails.

There remain two architectural features here to be referred to; the first, the ancient stone crosses of Ireland. These crosses have so appealed to the imagination of late that the world is being filled with them. Everywhere, in cemeteries and in many instances elsewhere, these crosses are being reproduced in vast numbers. This is one case in which a modern trend seems to have caught up a quaint and important architectural detail in no respect objectionable.

The crosses at Monasterboice and Tuam, and elsewhere, are all of intense interest. They record, or are intended to do so, all important human history. They begin with the creation and come down to the time of their erection. Those events counted salient in the Old Testament, the life of Christ in the New Testament, and incidents in the lives of the earliest saints, are all shown forth. The cross is literally covered on both sides and both edges, in every part, with sculpture. The form of the cross itself is highly effective. Inscriptions on some of these crosses show that they have stood about a thousand years. Their size is often impressively great, looming skyward to the pretentious height of about thirty feet. They are distinguished from the English market cross by their inscriptions, and by their greater proportions, and of course also by their more ancient character. They have been seized on in the public imagination as the most characteristic feature in Irish architecture. They symbolize more to the ordinary traveler than anything else. They were erected from mixed motives, of course, like all important works. In part they were commemorative of the builder or of some person whom it was desired to honor. In part they were a devotional sermon in stone, like a continuous prayer. They expressed, or were intended to express, the human acceptance of divine methods, and were supposed to show forth the dominance of God in the course of human history. It is probable that the vast majority of such crosses has vanished. There are relics, or at least, bases of crosses in a very great number of the towns of Ireland. In some cases the shaft is broken half off. In some cases the sculpture has worn away through winds and sand blasts. One can re-create a picture of Ireland when the crosses were most numerous. They were found upon the churches and in the cemeteries and in every market place. People lived in the immediate presence of the symbol of redemption.

Antiquarians have not yet solved all the problems connected with Irish crosses. Some of the sculpture is so far defaced that it cannot be certainly known for what it stood. Particularly the inscriptions, which are in a state of dilapidation, fail to give the explanation that was intended. What genius first designed and elaborated the Irish cross can probably never be known. We owe him a great deal. He has stamped all Ireland with a distinguishing feature, marked by reverence and artistic imagination. Here and there ruined crosses have been restored, and it is an effort much to be commended. These symbols stand for the best of old Ireland. They perhaps mean more in Irish history than any symbol can express in any other nation. This is the more true, as it is obvious that the erection of these crosses sprang from fine impulses, and that in many cases the crosses were wrought out by men of slight resources and meager training, but whose fine devotion led them to grope after the devotional and artistic expression shown by the crosses. They are not the finished and elegant work of the *dilettante,* nor are they the expression of a courtly life desiring to raise perfect monuments to itself. They arose out of the heart of the people.

The other architectural feature to consider is the round tower of Ireland. It is found not seldom in regions now remote from human habitation. Perhaps the largest is on an island off Galway. These towers in their original state were always lofty, and sometimes rival the elevation of large church spires. Their stone structure is put together in a manner denoting their great age, and is peculiar to Ireland. The entrance is always by a door set high above the ground and to be reached only by a ladder, which ladder could be drawn up after one. Their tops are sometimes battlemented and in other instances are conical. They are never of great diameter, like a castle keep, but their general impression is one of slenderness. They taper slightly. It is obvious from their small interior area that they were not intended to protect great bodies of people, and of course they could not be a refuge for animals. Many explanations have been attempted for these towers, none of them quite satisfactory. The usual judgment is that they constituted a retreat into which the sacred vessels or records or most valuable possessions of the church near at hand could be taken in time of danger. They would protect a few people with such treasures, and might also afford room for food during a somewhat extended siege. We do not know whether ample provision for water was made. It would seem that they were useful more as a refuge from sudden alarms, or marauding parties, than for any other purpose. It is likely also that they served as watch towers. We know that the Saxons had watch towers on the tops of which they also burned beacons. As watch towers, or as temporary refuges, we can see that they would have a reason for being. Nevertheless, there is just that sufficient degree of mystery in connection with them to render them still more attractive than they could otherwise be. An old stone edifice without a mystery is not of much use in the world. If we cannot have a secret stair or an ancient legend connected with the cause of the erection of such an edifice, or some glamour of romance, what is the use of the age of stone?

We sometimes become impatient with people who want all mysteries explained. They would be miserable if they had their wish. Life would be a bore if we understood everything. Happily, there is no danger of that condition coming about. Who built the bridges and the crosses and the towers and the castles, where the subterranean passages run, and why, are among the questions which it would be a great pity to have answered. Of course we wish to work on these matters and learn a little. It is no small part of the joy of life that the revelation of one mystery brings into view two greater mysteries. Thus we are amply provided with material for investigation. The source of romance and imagination, and the dear terrors with which we flirt, will never be exhausted. The delight of the world is that there is always a hill behind which we cannot see. We want to surmount it, and probably shall not rest until we do surmount it, but we should feel very miserable if there were not a greater hill beyond it.

Ireland indeed exists largely in our thought as a charmed land, a land in which the strange monsters or fairies of past ages had a share in the development of the present. St. Patrick's contest with the serpent is a general symbol of a rising, glowing spirit, fighting down the sinuous and treacherous elements on the destruction of which depends any fine civilization.

The warfare in Ireland between its northern and southern kings is not too remote to give a cast to its landscape. Old Tara still has its suggestive ruins, and the discovery of an ancient map has enabled us to trace such foundations as to make clear the reality and importance of that age when it was the center of Irish civilization. To the listening soul the harp still sounds upon its green hill, and its marching knights go out to enforce the precepts of order and decency.

Man can never rest in a state of chaos. At last the jarring elements of a race will pull together. The present era may be that in which all the Irish of every land shall unite to restore, embellish and glorify whatever is worth while in the past's history of mysterious, poetic, prophetic Ireland. Indeed, the Irish race is sufficiently numerous, wealthy and imaginative, to own and use Ireland as a kind of idealistic expression of the Irish character. The cross, the church, the homestead, the love of the home acres, the bridges, expressive of human co-operation and fellowship, the mountains, the loughs, mirroring heaven's blue, and every feature, natural and cultural, of old Ireland, may be correlated by some masterful man or men, till the whole island stands as an embodied ideal. The humdrum reader may pish at such statements, but the history of mankind and the unquenchable love for ideals indicate a better Ireland. I will never believe that an island with such a climate, such mountains, such streams, such verdure, such saints, and such opportunities, can fail to become tenfold more beautiful and noble. As England in its best estate symbolized certain ideals and the best human expression of them, so Ireland, taking advantage of its present opportunity, ought to become the shrine of the Irish race. Not merely must its sod be loved as most men in their normal state love soil, but out of that love as a basis we confidently anticipate will rise a far more glorious Ireland. There is room in Ireland for rest resorts to feed the hearts of millions who love noble scenery, where here and there stand the monuments of past struggles and heroic faith. There is room in Ireland for an endless development through the use of its abundant waters, at least a hundred-fold beyond the present stage of their use. There is room in Ireland for an architecture, so crowning each strategic location as to express everywhere the answer of man to the suggestions of the mountains and the arches of the forest. There is room for artistic expression in every art. There is a climate favorable to labor and to thought. As the location of the last outpost of Europe and the springing ground for a leap to America, Ireland should be the interpreter of the old world to the new, and the new world to the old. Neither time nor leisure permits the development of the reasons for what may seem to be vain imaginings. But once let a fine emulation, a spirit of harmony, touched by a spirit of sacrifice, prevail among the Irish people, as it must at last prevail, if we believe that God is in his heaven, and these imaginings are not too extravagant. Almost, as we write, we see that a tentative movement is being made to establish a line of steamers between western Ireland and America, to revive in a bay of Ireland a commerce which has been receding for hundreds of years.

THE MOST BEAUTIFUL SPOT IN IRELAND

THE road from Glengariff to Kenmare stretches across the beginning of the peninsula which is so beautiful that if the fabled Atlantis toward which it points is anything like this portion which still remains above ground, we have lost much of the best of the world. The drive from Glengariff on the southern shore of this peninsula, while abounding in splendid outlooks, is very different from the aspects met along the

northern shore. At a point seventeen miles west from Kenmare is a series
of inlets from the Kenmare River. The wide estuary is altogether salt
water, and the river which comes down under the suspension bridge at
Kenmare is a comparatively small stream which the name of the river
has carried out to sea. The inlets of which we speak form several loughs.
The elements of beauty produced here are abounding in number and in
grace of outline. To begin with, the variety of shore line afforded by the
incoming and outgoing of the tide is a marked attraction. Without ex-
posing any offensive tide flats, the receding tide reveals little islands of
stone. The coloration of the rocks is something fit to distract an artist.
Whether this color is caused by something in the rocks themselves on
which the sea water reacts, or is altogether due, as it certainly is in part,
to the seaweed, mosses, and lichens, we are uncertain. At any rate, there
is an unbelievably beautiful effect produced about the rocks, and this
effect is multiplied in its beauty by the irregular contour of the rock itself.
Ordinarily any bay is unsightly at low tide. One would say that this
lough is more attractive at the ebb than at the flood of the tide. Pictures
in either case differ so much that the dweller on these shores is gifted with
two scenes daily, although he looks morning and evening in the same direction. The lough kisses the feet of several mountains, splendid in their
rising lines. About them, continuing along the shore, there are wooded
hills, and here and there broken cliffs. On another side a lush meadow
falls gradually into the waters, and the long water-grasses wave. Patches
of seaweed, not in a monotonous line, but coming to the surface here and
there, make their contribution to the general effect. The scene is at its
best, not in a moment of absolute calm, but when a zephyr quietly caresses
the face of the waters so as to cause a broken, soft reflection of the mountains. Looking across the most interesting lough, one sees on a natural
terrace an attractive cottage with thatch and the surroundings of a substantial homestead.

The lower slopes are green with grasses or potato and grain fields.
Rising a little, we have shrubbery, and, on the greater heights, there is

stone of various tints, tending to gray and brown, with shadings of green. The blue and gray sky, the green, blue, and purple water, the green, in a dozen shades, of the vegetation, and the browns and grays of the protecting mountains, all touched off by the numerous rocks painted with their tide marks, offer us an array of more elements of beauty than I have ever seen elsewhere. I anticipate with pleasure the difference of opinion which such a statement is likely to call forth; but for me this region is superlative. Although it is not the grandest scene in Ireland, it is by no means lacking in grandeur. Its extent, while ample, is not too great to take in at once. The protective sense, so eloquent in pictures, is here. All shades of color are present. The domestic element is furnished by the farmhouse. There is positively nothing superfluous. There is, on the other hand, nothing lacking. From day to day, with the changing heavens and the rise of all the winds and the tides and the varying seasons, one should find here at least as many strikingly different pictures as there are weeks in the year. The Bay of Naples is always haunted by the sense of subterranean terrors, and it has not the softness and luxuriance of the Irish climate. The fiords of Puget Sound are more monotonous, while those of Norway are more cold and awful. The beauty of our scene is enhanced because it extends about the sides of an amphitheatre. It does not suggest loneliness or inaccessibility. While abounding in elements of strength, it is restful. There is a combination of majesty and grandeur, and an appeal to human feeling as well as to the eye of an artist. This wonder does not appear at its best in the picture entitled " A Hillside Farm," on page 111, but even there, on the right, the markings on the rock are seen, and the dreamy reflections. I like this view better than the severer terrors of the north and west Atlantic coasts of Ireland. And the cliffs, like a plummet which drops from the headlands into the sea, lack the winning quality. Looking down the vale of Glengariff, one sees what we gladly admit is a scene of arresting splendor. But there the sea is distant. Bantry Bay is a panorama of glory, but it is not so intimate and dear. The view from Queenstown shows some few cultural features which we should wish removed, and the background is not so impressive as this of which we speak.

HUNGRY MOUNTAIN——COUNTY KERRY

ACROSS TO THE PINES——COUNTY CORK

GALWAY BEAUTIFUL

GIANTS' CAUSEWAY—COUNTY ANTRIM

CARRIGADROHID CASTLE—COUNTY CORK

GLENARM—COUNTY ANTRIM

UNDER CROAGHPATRICK, CONNEMARA

There are harbors or inlets reaching into this peninsula from Kenmare River, which are only second in beauty to that here more fully described. Four bays, that of Ballydonegan, Cullagh, Ardgrooin, and Kailmakailloge, the two latter usually called harbors, and a series of little lakes only eight miles from Kenmare, are five centers of superb scenery. The background of all these scenes is the Caha mountains, called in their subordinate extension the Slieve Miskish mountains. If one for a moment turns his back on these scenes, although it is difficult to do so, and looks across the Kenmare river, he sees over the intervening three or four miles of water another range of mountains on the next peninsula north. They also are superb, and afford many fine outlooks particularly as we near Kenmare on our return, where the estuary narrows. In this latter region, also, we come upon splendid roadside trees, running off into narrow forests on either side, to the mountains' bases and to the estuary. It has not been without wisdom that a summer resort is established near Kenmare. We believe that it was about the drive from Glengariff to the lakes that Thackeray expressed his highest encomiums of Irish scenery. It is refreshing to have him give attention to such things and to leave the sore and quarrelsome spots alone for a time. Thackeray was almost too human. It would sometimes seem that if there was trouble anywhere, he wan'ed to be at the spot, and that he exhibited in his trip through Ireland certain of the characteristics of which the Irish have been unjustly accused, joy in a scrap. I am under the impression that Thackeray did not make journeys out on the peninsulas, a half dozen of which reach like fingers westward from the Irish coast. His comments seem to confine themselves to the main route along the bases of these peninsulas. He believes that all the artists of the world ought to be pensioned while they are sent for long studies in western Ireland. His praise is just, and expressed as only Thackeray could express himself in relation to the parts which he saw. I believe he would have thrown up his hands in despair had he made some of the journeys down these peninsulas. The only feature lacking as one looks toward the waters is a white sail. These waters ought to be dotted with yachts and cat-boats, and every conceivable modern device for enjoying the summer harbors of Ireland.

THE TREES OF IRELAND

OF OLD, we have thought of the trees of Ireland as having the oak as their king. A notable phrase in Macaulay speaks of the old hall of William Rufus, where the arches of Irish oaks resounded to the sonorous periods of Burke at the trial of Warren Hastings. Until this moment I never connected the Irish origin of the speaker with the similar origin of the arches, but it is significant. Curiously enough, however, the beech tree seems to belong to the rising dynasty of trees in Ireland. In speaking with certain persons wise in forest lore, I learned that the beech is steadily crowding out the oak, and that in certain regions where the oak was common fifty years ago, the beech now reigns almost supreme. Of course the oak is a tree that feeds the heart seeking after permanance and power. But if its reign must pass away, we know of no tree to which we could more heartily pay our new allegiance than to the beech. The boles are as smooth as the buttonwood, and sometimes as huge; and with its kind disposition to drop delicious nuts in the forest pathways, with its cheerful brightness and its highly useful timber, the beech has so much to commend it that it is no small addition to the pleasure of an Irish tour. One notices it as a border tree on highways, and in estates, and in paths and by streams. Its proportions in Ireland are often majestic. It is sometimes covered with moss and occasionally with ivy, but it is one of the trees which we like best without any adornment beyond its own beauty. We were pained in the case of one estate to see the beeches pruned high, a great many of their lower limbs having been removed, leaving merely tufts at the top, in order to obtain vistas. It were better to cut them down entirely than to disfigure them in this fashion. As a man with his arms lopped off, so these trees pained us to gaze upon them. We should not mention such an incident were it isolated. We have taken advantage of these splendid trees in our pictures. Indeed, without the beech, Ireland would scarcely know itself.

The oak has been sought out under English dominion since it is adapted, or is supposed to be adapted, to certain kinds of construction which can scarcely go forward without it. It is a great pity — perhaps we should use some stronger phrase — to destroy those oaks with short trunks which have very little marketable timber, but are thereby more picturesque, in their sturdy dwarf habit and great gnarled branches.

The elm is scarcely distinguishable in its habits from the oak, in Ireland, although in America it is quite different. The feathered elm is the usual form of the tree in Ireland.

The lime, a tree unusual in America, but very beautiful and plentiful in Ireland, is a most pleasing roadside decoration. We have heard much of the birch in Ireland, but saw very little of it, and almost never observed the brilliant white or salmon bark that is so common in the northern United States. Forests of it we never observed. Evergreens do not form a large feature of the Irish landscape. This is as it should be, because they never thrive in rich soils. The larch, of which we have always thought as a beautiful anomaly among trees, since it appears like an evergreen in summer, but sheds its leaves, is found more or less. It is not important to notice specially those species which are found in Ireland chiefly as exotics. The palm is seen now and then in sheltered localities in the south and west, near the sea. Nowhere else in the world, perhaps, does it appear, except in rare instances in southern England, in connection with northern growths. No doubt whatever palms exist in Ireland are from human planting. There is need for more attention to the planting of trees in Ireland. A country, however, which is given up to small farming cannot afford a great number of shade trees apart from the highways. Parking of extensive lands belongs to an old order that is passing away, and happily passing. Measures are being taken for the afforesting of such parts of Ireland as are not fit for cultivation, but will produce trees. It would not impress the casual visitor that there was a great extent of such places.

The fruit trees of Ireland do not cover a relatively large area. In and about County Armagh there are commercial orchards, but in general the fruit trees have been greatly neglected. Our personal view is that the rainfall and humidity of Ireland are not favorable to the highest success with orcharding, but in the western interior, as at Armagh, these conditions are ameliorated.

The hawthorn is a tree which flourishes without attention, fills the hedgerows, and is scattered along the borders of the brooks and adds materially to the beauty of the spring landscape. At its best estate, as on pages 81 and 112, it is as beautiful as, and more delicate than, the American dogwood.

The shrubs of Ireland, developing so luxuriantly as almost to reach the dignity of trees, call forth our admiration. Particularly the elder fills many a corner. It is amazing how many little nooks, even in a highly cultivated country, can be found where these volunteer decorations may disport themselves. Huge bushes of fuchsia are numerous in the hedgerows. They are found also clambering about the eaves of cottages, and in the corners of the walls.

The headlands that reach well into the sea are not well adapted for large tree growths. In such situations the mosses and the lowly flowers cling. There seems to be an arrangement by which every sort of soil and every exposed location is adapted to the nourishment of beauty. Even a cliff, which seems cold and bare to the careless eye, is covered with minute and beautiful growths.

OVER THE FARM—MOURNE MOUNTAINS

A KERRY SOUND

THE MOUNTAIN ROAD—COUNTY KERRY

A SCORE OF WALLS—COUNTY GALWAY

ABOVE MELLIFONT ABBEY—COUNTY MEATH

A CLIFDEN ROAD—COUNTY GALWAY

MET AT DUNLOE—COUNTY KERRY

THE VILLAGE MEADOW—SNEEM

ABOVE THE LOUGH—COUNTY KERRY

A RIVER CASTLE—COUNTY CORK

LICHEN BROOK—COUNTY KERRY

ROCKS AND REEDS—COUNTY KERRY

A PASTURE ON THE LEE

THE MIDDLE KILLARNEY LAKE—COUNTY KERRY

A BAY FARM—COUNTY CLARE

ACROSS KILLARNEY—COUNTY KERRY

CENTERS FOR SIGHTSEEING

DUBLIN is in itself a beautiful city, and is in the center of an attractive region. We have of set purpose in this volume omitted as a rule the well known conventional architectural features of the great cities. In touring Ireland, we found it best to make centers and return to them at night. From Dublin one may go a little to the northeast for twenty or thirty miles, as to Trim, and then swing southwest for five or ten miles, coming back to Dublin, thereby securing a good impression of rich agricultural Ireland. The region is not lofty, and it is so near town that a good many of the quainter rural features have vanished, but it is important as showing the transition of Ireland. Another journey may be made more nearly due north and about the same distance, after which one may swing shoreward and come back from the northeast. Such a journey would include Swords, Malahide, the hill of Houth, Ireland's Eye, and a great many features of importance. This journey should be made on a good day. The little church of St. Doolagh, the most interesting small church in Ireland, the towers at Swords, page 79, are included in this tour. Going southwesterly from Dublin and coming back from the south, one gets into the region of the Dargle, and in a part of the journey passes over the bare Dublin mountains, which, with their green intervening valleys, are most impressive. By varying the roads somewhat a second excursion in the same general direction may be made, for a second day. The most attractive and best-known scenery around Dublin is to the south. One may spend several days and find pleasant resorts on the shore at luncheon time, unless one has luncheon from the motor-car. There is on the coast near Bray a cottage whose features have been preserved, and whose beauties have been extended from generation to generation. We show it on page 87. A wholly different aspect appears on page 69. Of course this is not a typical Irish cottage. It is too good. But it is a valuable example indicating to what a cottage may grow. From every aspect it is charming, and the occupants were very gracious to permit us to do our work. Up and down Bray and its environs are numerous gardens and characteristic cottages. A little back of the town is a dwelling the roof of which is entirely covered over with clematis of the large variety.

When one finally leaves Dublin perhaps it is best to follow the coast closely, passing through Bray. Fine streams abound on this route, many of which we have pictured. The tour leads one into County Wexford, a region not of outstanding importance for striking scenery, but notable for its simple and attractive farm scenes. Wexford is a very old town, fought over by many races. On the journey from Dublin to Cork it is perhaps decided to go through in a day, following the shore, and then returning part of the way to examine in detail the beauties of the region. Following from Wexford to Waterford, one reaches that chief point, the confluence of three notable rivers, the Suir, the Barrow, and the Nore. This spot is distinguished, especially in the minds of those to whom the meeting of waters appeals, but there are no sharp elevations, and the writer was not so much impressed as he hoped to be. Possibly the dullness of the day may have accounted for it. One must always recognize that certain distant scenes and panoramas are most delightful to gaze upon for long periods, though rather impracticable in pictures. Waterford is a center not to be neglected. The variety of the drives from this city exceed in number our ability to count on the fingers of both hands, and almost all the drives are charming. One should go down to Traymore Bay. He will find many cottages in which the early furniture of hundreds of years ago is still intact. He will pass by noble trees and at last come to a far-reaching shore of diversified interest. We will say that the traveler has come from Wexford to Waterford. In this case it is important to make the journey from Waterford to New Ross and back half way to Dublin through Enniscorthy, as far as Gorey, thence proceeding to Newtownbarry, and from there over the mountain roads to New Ross. Even so, there is still a region to be investigated north of New Ross, as soft and sweet a valley as any in Ireland, running up to Leighlinbridge and Carlow, whence one may return by a parallel road to Leighlinbridge, and then through Thomaston to Waterford again. We followed the route also from Waterford in a generally western direction through Carrick-on-Suir to Clonmel, and thence to Fethard and Kilkenny, and so back through Kells to Carrick-on-Suir, whence one may keep on directly south and reach the shore road for Cork. The river Barrow has not the bold banks of some of the Irish rivers, but in certain of its reaches it cannot be surpassed, especially from Leighlinbridge to New Ross. The good roads of Ireland would easily occupy one for six months, even if the minor roads were neglected. There is, for instance, a route from Dungarvan on the shore, about a third of the way from Waterford to Cork, through Cappoquin to Lismore, and Fermoy, and thence southerly to Cork.

The Blackwater is a long stream, and in its course includes every sort of scenery. Lismore is a famous region, partly because it is near the seat of the Duke of Devonshire. The natural beauty of the country, aside from the numerous architectural remains, is engrossing. This journey includes numerous abbeys and castles, whose walls are laved by the passing streams. We journeyed also from Lismore directly over the Knockmealdown Mountains to Clogheen, which we reached on a feast day, and found crowded with people. The contrast between the lonely mountain road, where for miles we met no one, and the teeming city, was sudden and pleasing.

The route from Clogheen over minor roads to Cahir may be followed, or if one goes back through Clonmel, and thence north to Cashel, he will reach an ancient town of the first importance historically and architecturally. It is at Cashel on its citadel-like rock that church and castle, together, form one of the most satisfactory sky outlines in Ireland. I have said that many will wish to go from Dublin to Cork in a single day, but if proper quarters can be found, as is feasible at Waterford, a stay there will enable one to investigate the best region, so far as river scenery is concerned, in Ireland. Cork, the second city in the Free State, is also perhaps the second city where one may make his headquarters for a week or so. The harbor at Queenstown in good weather presents a great many varieties of outline. It is indeed the only portion of Ireland that many see. The transatlantic steamers in rough weather must enter the harbor, although they cannot go to Cork. We would not in any particular detract from the splendor of these scenes. We would only say that being the scenes most familiar to the traveler, they are on that account perhaps most celebrated. However, one should follow the stream by a smaller vessel to Cork itself, and thus secure in the inner lough a more intimate view which is entirely hidden from the harbor.

Nomenclature in relation to the portions of Ireland that has obtained the sanction of custom is: from the region of Cork and beyond to the south-west and thence north, perhaps to the County Galway, called the South of Ireland. North beyond that point on the west coast is called the West of Ireland. The terms are somewhat arbitrary and certainly indefinite, but one should thoroughly understand them, so as not to be led astray. Cork, then, is the center of the South of Ireland. It can care for most of the needs of civilized man. In spite of the baptism of fire and flood to which it has recently been subjected, it is still a great city with many architectural features of delight. Its great cathedral and various Protestant churches and public edifices are worth careful attention. On the romantic side the church, giving a name to " The Bells of Shandon," will not be overlooked. That enlivening and patriotic poem is known wherever the Irish race goes or indeed where English is spoken. Somebody has called it doggerel, but we wish the genial priest who wrote it had given us more. To be sure, it is not Tennyson, but it is better for most of us.

An interesting short excursion from Cork is to Kinsale, whose harbor, so picturesque from every aspect, we joyed in picturing. One may go by the main route and return through the narrower roads passing some of the sweetest rural landscapes in Ireland. All along this south coast to Bantry Bay there is an abundant interest for the lover of beauty. Running north from Cork to Mallow or farther there is an agreeable return journey

MOUNTAIN GLORY

BALLINSKELLIG BAY——COUNTY KERRY

A CARAGH LAKE FARM——COUNTY KERRY

AN ATHLONE DOOR—CO. WESTMEATH

A GOOD OMEN——COUNTY DOWN

CRAGS OF ANTRIM

A KILLARNEY BRIDGE

KILLARNEY WATERS—COUNTY KERRY

THE BROADS OF THE BROOK—COUNTY CORK

through the mountains, either west or east from Mallow. The route to Killarney may be taken in any one of three directions from Cork.

The doorway is through Macroom, with its picturesque castle at the bridge. Most travelers, however, follow the main western road from Cork through Bandon to Bantry. However pressed one is, it is advisable to turn south at Drimoleague, to Skibbereen, and thence on to Baltimore. This road is one of the most delightful in Ireland, going even south of Baltimore and reaching the great white beacon, a conical tower on the main opposite the island of Sherkin. The view of this beacon, and from it, appealed to me as much as anything that I have seen. It would be a delight to boat in these waters among the islands for a long time, but as a group of these islands are absolutely called the Catalogs, so any description of them would seem like a catalog. Baltimore has been said, how truly I know not, to have been the origin, at least in name, of the American Baltimore, through Lord Baltimore. In any case, the river which is followed in this route is, though short, full of all grace. It is far better to take a second day, either from Cork or from Glengariff, which latter point is near at hand, to explore the region south of Bantry Bay. This bay has a wonderful reputation for its beauty and its harbor facilities. At its head lies Glengariff Harbor, a minor arm of the main bay. There is no more delightful drive in Ireland than that between Bantry and Glengariff, although it is not so celebrated as that from Glengariff north. A second way to reach Glengariff from Cork is to branch southwest from Macroom, and make directly for Bantry Bay.

Glengariff vies with the lakes as being a center of interest and splendor in south Ireland. The drive from Glengariff on the southern shore of the peninsula directly west of it is full of thrilling scenes, as one edges along between the cliff and the waters. Coming at length opposite Berehaven and the island of the same name, where a port has been reserved by treaty with Great Britain, we reach Castletown, distinguished among peninsula towns as a remarkable center for beauty. It has the further advantage of being sufficiently far from the usual routes of travel to afford rest. At

Castletown one may go still west on the peninsula, or may turn directly north and return by the northern shore, which we have described in a special chapter, on the most beautiful spot in Ireland. From Glengariff again, one should cover at least a second time the route to Bantry, and without fail at the time of high tide. Both the nearer view-points and the more distant are distinguished, and feed the heart of one who loves the out of doors in a large way. Indeed, Glengariff usually holds the traveler who comes to know it. There are numerous by-roads and walks which cannot be ignored if one would see the sweet little dells of southern Ireland. Always, behind or in front, are the blue mountains and the blue sea. One could be content to live always at Glengariff if he were engaged in the work of an author or an artist.

The celebrated road leading from Glengariff to the Killarney Lakes and called after the Prince of Wales (because it is said to have been built during the time of trouble, when work was scarce and food had to be sent in), should be covered more than once. Perhaps the view of Glengariff Bay on the return route is unsurpassed in its way. It is a good road, though not well protected at the sides, but not fearful to one who travels leisurely, as all sane people must. In this connection, those who love motoring will be happy in Ireland, because even on the main roads there is little travel as compared with our American roads. When we consider the wonderful beauty of this region, and see that a few hotels of very moderate extent can care for all the travelers, and that these travelers are soon gone, coming only in the summer, one's amazement grows. There is no element of grandeur or of beauty lacking on this route. As one rises to the summit two or three highway tunnels convey one to the northern watershed drained by the Sheen river, a small but beautiful winding stream.

We have previously referred to Kenmare as a center for tourists. In this village is a cottage said to have been built for the poet Moore, but whether he ever occupied it, we do not know. It was fairly decorated with roses on our visit, and we recorded its charm.

Leaving our main route to the lakes, we follow westerly along the north bank of the Kenmare River to Sneem, perhaps pausing for a day in Parknasilla. Here is a maze of islands, and great care has been exercised to render the natural attractions accessible. Sneem has a bridge so picturesque that we must needs view it from all sides. Just at the upper side between an old ruin and a church, a pool in the meadow forms a satisfactory setting for a composition. One may return from Sneem by the minor route, which enters the main road for the lakes a few miles north of Kenmare. The route is to be recommended for its quiet, remote beauty. Yet the route from Sneem west to Ballinskellig Bay is too important to be missed. At Waterville one passes between fresh water and salt water to another small extension of the peninsula, and comes opposite the island of Valencia, a storied and worthily celebrated region. Perhaps it was a bit of Atlantis. Why not?

Proceeding northwest to Killorglin and Killarney, one certainly should come to rest after a long day, even if the day is begun at Kenmare or Parknasilla. Killarney is of course recognized as a center, and to many the only center, for sightseeing in Ireland. It is a great mistake, however, to confine one's attention to so small an area, however beautiful it may be. From Killarney southerly to Kenmare is pictorially the best route the author has ever covered. There is a picture at every turn of the waters, or a new aspect of the cliffs, and the reader may be very sure that he will turn often, as the road is the most crooked one that it has ever been my fortune to pass over. I would like to see some person wise in direction, who is able to keep that sense, and to know which way he was heading on this journey.

The little lakes of the region are just as attractive as the great lakes. The trees are superb, although perhaps tree growths as fine in number and beauty are to be found about Glengariff. The views of the upper lake are a vision of wonder, which must leave all men poor who have not seen it.

There are hostelries situated in full view of the lower lake, the outlooks from the windows of which are perfection. One of those views in this volume was made from the window of a hotel. Perhaps the little castle

of the McCartys, now ruinous, on a miniature peninsula, offers as good a
foreground for a lake view as can be had.

The swans are an important detail in all the water life of Ireland, and
an endless source of pleasure, though at times they are too insistent upon
their rights. A pair of swans at this landing, circling about with their
cygnets, were careful not to allow the most benignant intruder to come too
near. At the Glengariff hotel landing, also, there was a pair with their
young. They nested on an island a long stone's throw from the shore.
When the tide goes out, they delight in wading in shallow, inflowing fresh
waters, and picking up delicious tidbits; but on one occasion a party about
to take a boat ride was stopped for an hour and a half by the sturdy opposition of the father of the family. The hotel proprietor was called on to
help his guests. The swan stood before him, and reared his bill until it
was opposite the man's face. It was a case of " no thoroughfare." Meantime, the mother with her cygnets at a little distance, sailed about uncon-
cernedly, perfectly confident that she had an able protector.

The story that swans destroy all their cygnets above the number of
two may have some foundation, but we repeatedly saw three and four
half-grown cygnets following the parents. The dainty little creatures are
kept out all day at their lessons in foraging. School never lets out, yet
when the little ones are weary, they climb upon their mother's back, and
she folds her comforting wings about them in such a way as to make a little
nook or cubby where they rest and ride to their heart's content. Their dear
little heads and bright eyes are seen peeping out above the wings at times,
and at times they withdraw and their owners take long naps. The picture
is altogether delightful. As night draws on, the mother sails placidly away
with her young to the home island. The father, however, acts as patrol,
sometimes for hours, between the island and the shore, especially if he sus-
pects that some danger may lurk near. A swan with ruffled feathers, sailing about close in shore, and watching a suspicious person, is one of the
most beautiful sights in nature. It is said that swans on the Thames divide
the river so that a pair has its particular range and does not permit intru-

sion from any other pair. All about Ireland in favorable loughs, salt or fresh, and in the rivers, may be found swan families. They add a last touch of grace and charm to a water landscape, and it is not without reason that the artists of the Victorian period made much of these graceful creatures, as in the pictures in Godey's Lady's Book. The swan is a powerful bird, and it would be a daring creature that would attack it. They seem to make good their residence wherever they take up their quarters. An occasional feeding with bread crumbs induces them to live near the dwelling of the almoner, yet it is with much condescension that they accept favors. Even when they eat what one gives them, they appear to do so as conferring a favor.

Ross Castle is an edifice of fine architectural outlines whether viewed from the land, as we show it, or from the lake. The loftiest mountains in Ireland lie not far west of the principal lake, over the Pass of Dunloe. The variation of coloring in these mountains at morning and at noon and in the evening is so wide in range, and presents at each change so many new aspects of beauty, that one never tires of gazing. As one goes up and down the borders of the lakes, and the differing sky line rearranges itself, sometimes as clear as a cameo, sometimes entirely veiled, sometimes with cloud caps and not seldom with long fillets banding the peaks halfway to their summits, one is conscious that he is in the presence of mystery and beauty raised to its highest power.

Muckross Abbey, at the middle lake, lies in private grounds. It is more visited than any other ruin in Ireland, because it is convenient. Its location across gentle pasture fields, over the tops of hawthorn blooms and between noble trees, seems to have been pre-arranged for our admiration. Another aspect from the graveyard on the yonder side is well worth studying. The cloister and its garth are among the most interesting.

One may drive for four miles or more to the Dinas cottage, beyond the abbey. The way leads between magnificent beeches, and along the shores of the middle lake. Old bridges come to view. At length the waters narrow and we reach the famous Meeting of the Waters, which is not by any means the most beautiful aspect of the Killarney lakes. We surmise that the idea of the waters coming together has impressed people so that they presume the point is one of great importance. On this journey there is no return. One must pass out by another route, and go back to Killarney around the lake. The town of Killarney itself is more or less interesting, but its principal attraction for us was its rows of cottages, embowered with vines and flowers. The Killarney rose, now so fashionable, we did not find to be in special evidence here.

Happily, we can love a rose even when it has no name. There is a delight in picturing cottages because their inhabitants enter into the joy of it. I would never spoil my day in waiting about for permission to enter castle grounds. Where there is a gate keeper and an established fee that is well and good. We should not rashly conclude that fees are exacted to exploit old grounds or historic edifices. The expense of the upkeep of such places is very large. It is probable that the fees received seldom cover the expenses. At any rate, we cannot too often be reminded that a great war has left many persons in reduced circumstances, who were wealthy before. The poorest man you meet may be the lord of the manor, completely tied up by debts. Yet we do not mean to imply that an owner of a fine estate must be poor in order to excuse him for exacting fees. The American sometimes misunderstands these things. In our own country great estates are as a rule not accessible under any circumstances except through friendship with the owners. In Europe, there is at least a sense of trusteeship that leads the owners to make arrangements for public inspection under certain conditions.

The Cascade of the Torc is in time of high water an object of remarkable attraction. Even in times when little rain has fallen, the lighter veil of water is well worth seeing. The quiet stream, however, on the left as one goes toward Kenmare from Killarney, afforded us a great many compositions. Westward from Killarney, around the northern side of the lake, one comes upon an unusually extensive level plane, on the way to Killorglin. Going thence to Milltown, we find one or two abbeys, at the borders of that village, that hold our interest for hours. In one of them there is a great tree covered with ivy, and growing close to the old chancel, in the interior. As one looks past it at the mullioned east window, a composition of great beauty is afforded. We are on the way to Tralee, the most important center commercially in this part of Ireland, and a city of some architectural merit. This town again is at the root of another of those peninsulas, each a miniature empire in itself. Going from Tralee westward, to Castlegregory, and thence to Dingle, the road offers distinguished attractions. The latter part of the route at the present time is somewhat narrow, and it is perhaps better to diverge southwesterly, at Finglass River. The extreme western point of this peninsula, reached through Ventry, terminates in a very bold rise of land, and looks out toward numerous islands with a romantic past. It is possible to return from this journey on the south shore, for the whole distance, through Castlemaine, and so on either to Killarney or to Tralee.

From Tralee northward toward Limerick is a purely farming region. It is perhaps best to go through Newcastle. At Adare we find remarkable conditions. The lord of the manor here has had sufficient influence or wealth or strength of character to insure great cleanliness about the village and its environs. It is one of the model towns. Aside from its wholesome sweetness, the interest centers in the two remarkable ruins, those of the Franciscan Abbey and of Desmond Castle. The castle, in its extent and variety and location, is of the highest interest. The remains are not so scanty that we cannot re-form most of the castle life. It may be counted one of the best spots in Ireland to study the age of feudalism. The water gate, the various posterns, and the courtyard with its truly majestic and almost unique beeches, show the early features of a castle at its best estate. But we should say that the main entrance, where the drawbridge was and the portcullis fell, could hardly be surpassed anywhere for dignity and an effect of power. Within, the castle rises, tier upon tier, as it was modified in early modern times. Here the public may wander at will, simply procuring a ticket at the estate office, and from the castle we may go on to the

abbey. The maze of drives in these grounds leaves the stranger somewhat
at a loss, but I know no region where I would be more content to be lost.
There are at least four good aspects of the abbey from without, as seen
through the great beeches, or past a relic of the external wall and gate, or
from the other two points of the compass. The setting is even more pleasing than that of Muckross Abbey, though the extent may not be so great.
Small chapels, in the niches of which, with their pointed Gothic arches, lie
the effigies of old worthies, over which the luxuriant vines clamber, occur
at several points in the interior. A day spent at the castle and the abbey,
with the village inn as a base, or as an excursion from nearby Limerick, is
to be commended. We did not try the village inn, but it looked very in-
viting, and is evidently under the same enlightened management that has
wrought such wonders in the village at large.

Limerick's history is at times piquant, at times awful, but always interesting. It must be left to the historian. The city lies in one of the most
advantageous situations possible, at the head of the estuary of the Shannon
and at the beginning of the route up river leading to the extensive and
famous Lough Derg. The Shannon is a large stream through which an
immense body of water moves. The river is worthy of a continent.

It is worth while, on an extensive tour, to return from Limerick by the
shore route on the southern side of the Shannon to Listowel, and Bally-
bunnion. If one should come to Limerick from Tralee by the way of
Castle Island and Abbeyfeale, this route to Listowel would be new.

Limerick is an interesting center, second indeed in importance to Killarney, but for investigation of early Irish life, and the shores and islands
and abbeys of extensive Lough Derg one can hardly afford to miss it.
Limerick may also be used as a starting point for a journey of absorbing
interest to Tipperary, Cashel, Thurles, Nenach, and so back to Limerick.
Another journey directly eastward from Limerick, over the Slievefelim
Mountain to Thurles and thence north to Roscrea and Kirr, then Nenach
and Limerick by the way of Killaloe, does not repeat any of the previous
journey. Killaloe, at the foot of the lake and at the outgo of the Shannon,

IN IRELAND

CARAGH OVER THE TREETOPS—COUNTY KERRY

CROSS AT TUAM—GALWAY   A CROSS——MONASTERBOYCE

ST. BRIDGET'S WELL—CO. CLARE

A DONEGAL BYROAD

A DONEGAL CASTLE

MID-TIDE—CREAGH

has ever been an historic and romantic site. The city of Limerick itself has its " points of interest " which every one is ready to point out, and we need not dwell on them.

Proceeding now northward from Limerick to Galway, one passes through the last county of southern Ireland, which might just as appropriately be called western Ireland, only that is not its name. County Clare is that one in regard to which hands of horror are lifted up as men exclaim upon its extreme poverty and objectionable frontier quality in general. The fishermen on the coast of Counties Clare and Galway have suffered of late their worst and probably their finishing calamity in the unprecedented term of bad weather, which has left them practically without means of livelihood for two years. The consequence will probably be that the numbers of the fishermen will decrease more and more in a progressive ratio. They have been decreasing for a long time. Modern fisheries are carried on now more successfully in a larger way than by the old methods. Fishing has always been a precarious form of existence. We remember other good men of old times who toiled all night and took nothing, and who looked to One on the shore to make suggestions. Aside, however, from the fishers, the farmers' sufferings have been caused by long continued rains, but their fertile acres remain to them, and they will recover, and probably will thrive. In fact, we recollect no county in all Ireland where there was more beautiful cottage life. Farm after farm had its attractive homestead. Nor did it appear that the people were one whit behind the rest of Ireland in suavity and intelligence. One is reminded of the " away down East " idea in New England. New Yorkers look with more or less humorous tolerance upon the down easters, thinking of New England. When you reach Boston, you are told that down east is in Maine. But at Portland you are sent to the eastern part of the state, and there, if you inquire, men shake their heads and direct you to New Brunswick. But there the inhabitants do not consider themselves down easters, but send you on to Nova Scotia and Prince Edward's Island, until at last you reach the eastern confines of Newfoundland, and to get away down east, must leap off into the

Atlantic. In this continuous progress, each district looks with mild contempt upon that one easterly of it. So in Ireland, as we start from Dublin, they shake their heads as to the South of Ireland, thinking of Cork. At that city you are supposed to be going merely, with a kind of bravado, to see Bantry Bay and the lakes. As you look around in this last region for the bears to bite you and the robbers to spring upon you, you find yourself in the garden paradise of Ireland. But they tell you that County Clare is the limit both in the old meaning and the new. Arrived in Clare, you still find brotherhood and agriculture, quiet and pleasing fellowship, and every evidence that people consider themselves to be as they really are, in the center of the world. If, however, you converse a little with them, they will tell you that up beyond Galway on the west coast, and in Connemara, you reach a part of Ireland that is really out of the world, and beyond the consideration of rational men. So the process may go on, until you reach Sligo and Donegal and the extreme north. And all the way you find people with heads and two legs and with smiles and kindness, and a full quota of wits. They live in a beautiful land in no wise inferior to the regions south of them. In fact, were I to be a resident of Ireland, I think that Donegal has features as winning as any, to call one to it.

From Limerick through Ennis, one may pass directly to Galway, but to do so is to lose the wonders of the Cliffs of Moher, Liscannor Bay, and the bold road on the shore around Black Head, and so on through Kinvara to Galway. There are thus two routes, as usual, in life, and we are always distracted to know which way we should go. Of two good things, choose both. We passed from Ennis through Crusheen, and Gort, to Galway, and making that headquarters, returned later to explore the frontiers of Clare.

Galway is fairly considered the beginning of western Ireland, by which we mean really northwestern Ireland. It extends farther north than Antrim of the six counties. Indeed, the term Ulster is a far more precise designation than northern Ireland, for the six counties.

Galway was once more important commercially than at present. It supplied us with more pleasing farm and cottage scenes than any other section of Ireland. Lying as it does between Galway Bay and Lough Corrib, with a plains country of rich lands to the east, and the splendid scenic region of Connaught to the northwest, it is a very satisfactory place of residence for a long stay. Indeed, two or three hundred years ago it was regarded as an important center of culture, and its people as among the most enlightened of the British Empire. It still has its university. Our drives from this city have left a very pleasing impression. We went east to Athenry and thence north for twenty miles, through Tuam, and then into Cong and so back on the eastern shore of Corrib to Galway. We also journeyed from Galway northwest to Oughterard, and the region of the Twelve Pins, whence we made excursions by some of the byroads to the wild frontiers of the Atlantic, the most desperately stricken portion of Ireland.

We were told at Galway that the Aran Islands were suffering economically to an extreme degree. Undoubtedly measures will have to be taken to assist the fishermen to emigrate, or to take up other callings.

Regarding Lough Corrib, it shares with Lough Neagh, which latter is the largest body of fresh water in the British Isles, the disadvantage of being in a plains country with low banks. To an American, it is not so attractive as the mountain loughs, as of course we are not greatly impressed with the extent of the Irish lakes. Nevertheless, its extremely tortuous shores afford many lines of beauty, and miniature harbors without number.

On one of our excursions to Headford from Galway, we came upon a cottage of Michael Fitzgerald, the roses of which we thought wonderful. We returned the next morning and found the family surprised at our early hours of labor. One of the pictures of this dwelling we have honored with first place in this book. Another aspect of it appears on page 35. On many occasions, on this drive, the road crests a small hill, below which lie a village's roofs. Such roofs, in thatch or old mossy slate, are the pleasantest possible feature of man's work, especially as seen from above. To us they are more delightful than the view of a mountain range. This entire region, north of Galway and east of Loughs Mask and Corrib, is one of the most remarkable plains in Ireland. At one point there is a road six miles in length, without a hair's deviation to the right or left. Of course, in the process of ages, the land here has risen. It was once a part of the lake or the sea, which are not much below it. Claregalway, with its river, castle, and abbey, and many others not inferior in attraction, give us pause.

We have referred to Cong as the ancient seat of learning and ecclesiastical authority. On the border line between Galway and Mayo, a part of the village being in either county, and on the border also between Lough Mask and Lough Corrib, it is in the midst of features of remarkable interest, besides being the heritor of a strange history. The river here, connecting the loughs, is scarcely a mile in extent as we see it. The rest of it is under ground. It rises full grown in a great pool at the center of the village. Cong Abbey has a history so replete with interest that it has been treated in a special volume. At present its ruinous condition has been arrested by slight restorations. We show its most interesting side. On the river there is a stone fish house, of dainty architectural outline. In the old days the net at the weir was set and so arranged that it rang a bell at the abbey if fish became entangled in it, whereupon a monk would come down and secure the catch. Fishing rights on these streams, possessed by the monks, were a source of wealth, as the waters have always teemed with large salmon. Cong, as a center of culture, had a high place in the ancient day, and it was also enriched by lands, some of them lying at a great distance. The abbot was therefore an important political personage. Here kings and princes resorted, and the total population dependent upon or connected with the abbey, in some capacity, numbered several thousand.

The islands of Lough Corrib are of much interest, particularly the Holy Isle, where is one of the most ancient inscriptions in Ireland. It refers to a relative of St. Patrick, and is of the highest historical importance, making that great character real and near. There are also on this island remains of a small church, or oratory, coeval with the tomb. In good weather the journey to the island is delightful. One combines a sense of pilgrimage with the delights that nature affords.

LORD ARDILAUNE'S GATE—COUNTY GALWAY

A DRUID TREE—COUNTY KERRY

A KILKENNY HOMESTEAD—COUNTY FERMANAGH

KILLARNEY WINDINGS—COUNTY KERRY

LOUGH FINN

FEUDALISM—COUNTY ANTRIM

CASTLE GATE AND VILLAGE STREET

THE LEE DECKED FOR BRIDAL

OVER BALLYCASTLE FIELDS—COUNTY ANTRIM

AN ARCH AND A SPIRE—COUNTY FERMANAGH

THE VILLAGE HILL—COUNTY WATERFORD

AWAITING A BITE—COUNTY CORK

DUBLIN MOORLANDS

COTTAGE AND CHURCH—COUNTY SLIGO

A CROAGHPATRICK SHORE—COUNTY GALWAY

UNDER KILLARNEY MOUNTAINS

Galway is not easily left behind, but we must follow the gleam. As we go northwest, we skirt several small shallow lakes, with water lilies or water grasses. The shores of the river at Oughterard are bordered by marvelous beech groves. Onward past long and narrow lakes, like streams, we reach a fork where we may swing north into Joyce's country, between two mountain chains. This part of Ireland differs strikingly from any we have hitherto passed through. The valleys are narrow and the population is scanty, the arable land being meager, but the scenery! More and more we revel in it, until it is almost intoxicating. In bad weather the effect of these mountains would be extremely gloomy, and the traveler would feel himself at the end of the world. In such a lightsome day, however, as that on which we moved among them, we could almost caress their summits, so near and friendly and clearly defined were they. Going up from Weir bridge northerly past Lough Inagh, we have the Twelve Pins immediately over that narrow stretch of water. It is absolutely necessary, if we would know Ireland, to circle these mountains, and to do that one must find an abiding place for the night in or near Clifden, for this region is too beautiful, too varied, too extensive to pass by lightly. Just south of Clifden there is a region which is matched nowhere else in Ireland by the immense number of little lakes, many of them too small to be indicated on the map. Beyond Clifden is that parish which is said to have Boston as its next westward parish. The Connemara region alone might detain one for weeks, every waking hour of which could be spent in exploring the valleys or the lakes; for here, in a region twelve miles square, there is every possible element of Irish scenery. There is bold headland, shelving beach, landlocked bay, open ocean, bog, lowland lake, all presided over by the Twelve Pins which hide away some mountain waters. There are villages, there are farms and fisheries, and resorts for travelers. From whatever angle they are viewed, the central mountains of this district present an outline of such irregularity as to surprise one with every gaze.

When at length we journey north, either by way of Old Head or by the narrower inland road to Westport, Newport, and Mallaranny, we approach a country no less fair. There is no more impressive drive than that from Westport below Croagh Patrick on the left, with Clew Bay on the right, and so circling back to Killary Harbor and Leenaun. This town is named by good judges of scenery as surpassing. Killary Harbor, a long and narrow estuary, with mountains on either side, is the most perfect specimen of an Irish fiord. The mountains that rise here are loftier than most of the Irish mountains so near the sea. They are the advance guard, facing the Atlantic. With their crests nearly twenty-seven hundred feet above the sea which lies immediately below them, they have a majesty more impressive than many mountains that are loftier. The tide in these parts of Ireland has a wide range between high and low. It is often necessary to return to a view-point in high tide to secure the best effects. On the road to Clifden, past Kylemore Lough, the castle and church thereon are impressive, standing out in their light outlines against the solid green, and the lough itself is a perennial joy. At the risk of making comparison unpleasing to some, we venture in all good humor to say that western Galway ranks with the Killarney lakes and mountains, and with Glengariff.

A quiet and beautiful retreat is found at Mallaranny. It has the merit of being entirely detached from any town, and therefore it does not appeal to persons who are not happy in scenery alone. It does, indeed, look out on wide tide flats, and seems to have been unwisely chosen as a site in that particular. It may be, however, that this entire shore affords nothing better. It looks across to Croagh Patrick toward the south, and Curraun Peninsula on the west, and to a range of mountains on the northeast. It stands in the inevitable location dictated by the pass to the north. Off the shore, from Mallaranny to Westport the islands are strewn thickly. Going on west from Westport, we were happy in beholding Croagh Patrick from two angles. This mountain dominates the entire region, though Benbury on Killary Harbor is somewhat loftier. Croagh Patrick, however, stands by itself. Its associations with the saint are such that it is revered by the population in general, and stands as a great monument, always reminding them of their faith.

Driving west from Mallaranny, one reaches Achill Sound, beyond which is Achill Island, rising suddenly from the sea, and terminating on the extreme west with the most sheer cliffs to be found in all Ireland. It is not, therefore, without reason that the attractions of the island scenery have brought this portion of Ireland into prominence.

The journey from Mallaranny to Sligo may be made either east or west of Lough Conn. The eastern side shows more mountain features, whereas the western side is more generally a plains country. On reaching Ballina, a point to which one comes from either side of the lake, there are again two choices of route. The mountain road passes Lough Gleneask. The usual direct route follows the coast more nearly and skirts the foot of the uplands. Making a headquarters at Bundoran, one may explore from that region more lakes than from any other one quarter in Ireland, when we consider their beauty and variety. Lough Allen is not reached by the best roads, but they are entirely feasible. The lough lies between two ranges, with a third range at the north end.

Lough Gill, very near to Sligo, has been said by more than one good judge to be equal to the Killarney Lakes in beauty. I would rather say that it is not so impressive in the height of its surrounding hills, but that in itself it is fully as beautiful. One makes the circuit of the lough, and to acquire any fair knowledge of its beauties it is well to go around it in opposite directions on successive days, or go twice around it in the same direction the same day, in the morning and in the afternoon. We always wish to have the sun behind us in looking at any landscape, particularly one in which a lake appears.

The most ravishing view of a cottage we obtained on the south side of the lake only four miles from Sligo. The roses covered the gable of a barn as well as the sides of a house and shed, built on three sides of a square, a very unusual thing in Ireland. The picture was made in a drenching rain, but seems none the worse for that.

The route to Enniskillen from Bundoran by the southern or northern banks of Lough Erne, thence returning through Manor Hamilton and

Sligo, takes one over the line into the Ulster government, but a permit may be obtained for a day without difficulty. The route is marvelous for its lake scenery. It may be varied by turning northeast from Belco, and passing by Lough Melvin to Bundoran. The mountains in this part of Ireland are not so lofty as in Galway. We would say, however, that in our judgment a mountain with foliage, even if it be of very moderate elevation, is more beautiful than the bare loftier peaks. It requires both sorts to meet all our dreams. Ireland has both.

I confess to a very strong liking for this part of Ireland. About Sligo I found the farmers very intelligent, and better satisfied with their life than elsewhere in Ireland. One of these men was eighty-five years old, as straight as a pine tree, and being past the age of difficult manual labor, he wore a white collar. His speech was beautiful, both in its voicing and in its diction. His son, a man of middle age, was an enthusiastic farmer. He was experimenting with crops not usual in his region, and particularly was successful in garden products for the small city markets. He was not alone in intelligence and joy in his work. His neighbors were emulating his labors.

Leitrim, a small county, is an epitome of Ireland, so far as its contour is concerned. It has lake, mountain, and meadow, each at its best.

There is a narrow neck of land in this vicinity connecting the county of Donegal with the southern portions of the Free State, and it is in this part of Ireland that one must be careful about passing over back roads near the line, where no customs booths are placed. We should not be harsh in our judgments of the care exercised by the officials, because the state needs very much any revenue it may derive from customs, and if the government were at all slack on the border, they would be overrun with smugglers.

Continuing our northern journey, we find Donegal to be a lively city. One may go from this place by a very direct route to Londonderry, in Ulster. All travelers, however, will wish to go west from Donegal along the interesting shore of Inver Bay, McSwines Bay, and the Killybegs. The route west of this place, not leading to any large city, is not, especially on

A BISHOP OF TUAM   A THOUSAND YEARS AGO

A ROADMASTER'S COTTAGE—COUNTY DUBLIN

SKIRTING KILLARNEY LAKES—COUNTY KERRY

WHITE HORSE COTTAGE

ANTRIM'S EAST COAST

THE GARDEN PATCH—COUNTY SLIGO

ROSE COTTAGE—COUNTY GALWAY

the return journey on the northern side of the peninsula, a broad through track, but it is feasible, and has its attractions. The populations cover Donegal scantily. The county has much mountain land. Probably more of it is waste, in the agricultural sense, than is true toward the south. The mountain outlooks, however, are superb. One has the choice at Andara of driving past Lough Finn to Letterkenny, and so on past Milford to Rosapenna, or of going from Andara north and keeping the shore route, through Dunglow, the Rosses, and Dunfanaghy, and so on to Rosapenna. In these journeys one is almost alone with the natural world. The route past Lough Finn is the upper road, passing over a region which for many miles is seven or eight hundred feet above the sea. The shore route is altogether through lower land. To the west of Dunglow, lies Aran Island, and to the northeast of Dunfanaghy is Tory Island, holy in its memories and containing most interesting historical relics of early missionary work.

There are two dominating mountains in this county. Errigal, a little under twenty-five hundred feet, lies directly above the upper Lough Nacung, and in its general effect is of startling beauty. Standing almost alone, and viewed from Bryan's Bridge, near Gweedore Hotel, or at any point going eastward for some miles, it always has an effect of grandeur, as if it were a kind of guardian of the whole country. The other mountain is called Muckish. Its elevation is not quite so great. There is, however, a little body of water to the north of it which enables the traveler to see it to the best advantage from a small hillock. A little to the east is Glen Lough, most attractively seen from the west. Leaving Rosapenna, we were fascinated by the beauties of Mulroy Bay, but at high tide only. There is no more sweet and restful scenery in Ireland. Milford, reached by a tortuous hill, is a point from which the small peninsula to the west of Mulroy Bay may be investigated. One goes thence to Ramelton. We found here a row of dwellings with one-story porches, roofed in slate.

The coloring of the moss we recommend to any passer-by as something worth a record with his camera. It is the most fascinating porch we saw in Ireland.

With this cursory view, we conclude our itinerary of the Free State around a circuit of Ireland.

The cross routes to Dublin from Galway east, or from Sligo south to Athlone, may be followed. We tried them both. We also, running south from Sligo, went east from Boyle to Carrick-on-Shannon, and thence to Longford, and so on to Dublin. This last journey leads through a region of lakes with ramifying arms, between Carrick-on-Shannon and Longford.

The great central plain of Ireland is crossed by these routes. There are occasional bogs, but the greater part of the land has been drained, and in general the roads are interesting. Lough Ree, draining a large portion of the country north of Athlone, is really an enlargement of the Shannon. This stream, with its wealth of water, comes down into Lough Ree from Lough Bofin, and numerous loughs to the north. The Shannon, for the greater part of its course, flows through meadows. It is not so notable in a scenic way as some of the other rivers of Ireland, but commercially and economically it is of the highest importance.

Athlone is a typical inland city. All these cities are small, and most of them are either ecclesiastical centers, as Cashel and Armagh, or were located, as in Athlone, because of fords. Central Ireland is seldom seen by the tourist. It is true that one may go from Dublin by motor directly to the Lakes of Killarney through Mallow without visiting Cork. But the attractions of the coast are such that travelers usually prefer to follow it. Interior Ireland is therefore an unknown country to the traveler. Yet this interior is really the backbone of the state in an agricultural sense. The plain between Tullamore and Carrick-on-Shannon as the main east bounds, and Roscommon and Portumna as the main west bounds, is the largest low plain in Ireland. The plain to the east of Tullamore, and thence most of the way to Dublin, and north and south of this line for many miles, is somewhat more elevated, and perhaps more populous. There is a finer network of roads north and south of Naas and Kilcullen than is to be found elsewhere in Ireland, with the possible exception of Maryborough, some-what to the west. This extensive region is very thoroughly cultivated, perhaps we should not say intensively. The students of economic problems in Ireland are of the opinion that the state would sustain about a half million more people than at present on the land. We should say that with intensive agriculture the estimate is too small, because in many instances two crops could be raised instead of one on the same land. Farmers, however, often complain that their acreage is too small. It is too much to expect a great increase in the agricultural population of Ireland. There is room for a greater increase along industrial lines, which are now very much neglected. It is pitiful to see in southern Ireland mill after mill in ruins, and that not from being wrecked, but from neglect. The fiscal arrangements of long ago under the British government discouraged manufacture in Ireland, and in this region actually throttled it. The water powers of Ireland are not extensive, as judged by those of the northeastern or mountain states of America. They are, however, superior to those in Britain because of the more numerous mountains and the somewhat greater rainfall. This white coal of Ireland is mostly yet to be utilized. There is a great development in store for Ireland provided capital is once assured, as it is now becoming assured, that it is welcome and will be protected. It would not be surprising if the Irish of America should here and there, returning to Ireland, employ their acquired wealth in the development of manufactures in their old homestead. We found returned farmers and others who, having gained a competency, had engaged in mercantile lines. There are always enough merchants in any country, and a few which could be spared. The attractions of " storekeeping " are very great for persons who falsely believe, as many do in every generation, that it is only necessary to engage a shop, put in a stock of goods and sit at the receipt of custom. All over the world, including Britain and America, we find a multitude of lackadaisical, small, unnecessary shopkeepers. If one half of the shops were closed the world over, it would be better for their keepers and for the public. The buyer and the seller appear everywhere. The agriculturalist and the manufacturer need encouragement. Wise enterprise is the rarest quality in any state. One would say in America that billions had been

wasted in enterprises without a good basis.   Ireland would be rapidly enriched at the present time by enterprising men of judgment, who should
start industries to engage her unemployed labor, so that it might find at
home an ample use.   Power is more and more at a premium everywhere.
When we saw so many waters coming down from the mountains, and running idle to the sea, the thought would intrude that these waters would be
more beautiful if they were more useful.

INCIDENTS OF TRAVEL

THERE is a pretty general sympathy, sometimes wasted, shown toward
Americans traveling in Ireland, owing to their supposed thirst for
strong waters.   A major (recent) at a pretty cottage, begged us to come
in, and when we hesitated, he said, " Come, I will give you some fine whis-
key, something you can't get in your own country."   We still hesitated, but
the Irish are the soul of hospitality!   Our usual reply to such invitations,
which were not infrequent, was that we were good Americans, and that we
were trying to back up the spirit of our Constitution, as well as the letter.
We were often informed that Americans, as a rule, were not so punctilious.
Seriously, we believe that the thirst which Americans develop abroad is
overestimated.   It is true that your traveling American is sometimes seen
imbibing, in public, liquids which at home are taboo, but our judgment,
after seeing many traveling Americans, is that the American abroad lives
very much as he does in his home land.   He is not a natural hypocrite,
nor can he claim, as formerly he did, that the impure water in Europe
made it unsafe to drink.   Everywhere we drank unstintedly of such water
as the public faucets afforded, and nowhere did we suffer any ill effects.

It was not particularly pleasing, however, to learn that the most flourishing industry in Ireland, as in Scotland, is connected with brewing and
distilling.   Great Britain ennobles its brewers and distillers.   It is necessary
for the state to do this, as God has not.   Nor have the persons concerned.

Of course the European point of view about these matters is different from our own, but views have changed in America, and we believe that they will do so in Ireland. In the year 1800 in America it was not unusual for clergymen, if they made investments, to have shares in distilleries. We were informed with indignation by certain English ladies that they were continually bombarded through the mails with solicitations to take shares in enterprises for rum running into America. In these days, in America, the clergymen do not endorse the liquor interests.

We shall be glad to see the day when the manufacture of clothing in Ireland overtops the brewing interests.

It is undeniable that we became very thirsty on Irish roads. In southern Ireland, in a dry time, the dust contains some irritant, perhaps alkali, which made our mouths sore, when we were out all day on the roads. I suggested that a remedy would be to keep our mouths shut, and not to talk while we were motoring. Nevertheless, at night, a certain member of our party came in with a sore mouth.

A journey in an average year in Ireland would escape this difficulty, as, except in June, it is not likely to be dusty.

We really suffered at times for the lack of a drink of water. We would advise travelers to provide themselves with thermos bottles, which we never carried, having placed it before ourselves as an achievement to travel through Ireland obtaining our food and drink by the way. In this we succeeded, although at times with some hardship. Water is an article which is never given one at the table of a hotel except on special request. Americans are known to want water, but except in the rarest instances they are expected to ask for it. The American habit of placing a glass of ice water before a guest at a hotel would cause a shudder in any Irish or English landlord.

We can, however, without the slightest degree of prejudice through partiality for the Irish, testify that we saw very few people drunk in Ireland. There would be days at a time when we saw no one under the influence of liquor. The exception was usually at the close of a market day, when the farmers were returning. Then, occasionally, one would see a sad-featured wife driving, while her lord and master lopped beside her, unable to hold the reins. Of course, with the public houses as numerous as they are in Ireland and in Britain, there must be a great deal of drinking. If the money that went in this direction went to the improvement of the homestead and home acres, a transformation would occur in a few years. The staggering debts of all the British Isles could be carried without danger of a break were Father Matthew's preachings heeded. He is properly re-membered with a monument, and his memory is loved, and the work that he did in encouraging temperance is still having its effect.

In our shopping in Ireland we found that bread is always cheaper, and often better, than in America, although the wheat is largely imported. There is a powerful trend in Europe to keep the necessities of life at a low price. This spirit appears in southern Ireland in the universal feeling that house rents should be very low. Probably the Irishman who has bought his land under the Land Act thinks of his payments as for land and not for a dwelling.

In North Ireland, particularly in Belfast, there is a system of municipal building by which the rent of many persons is almost canceled. It would surprise the American workingman if he knew that a very good tenement could be obtained in Belfast for six shillings a week. Of course labor is paid much less than in America, but the system of rentals does much to balance the difference between the countries. It is true that this method of absorb-ing the rent in the taxes is pure socialism. The question is too big to discuss here. I can only say that I believe it to be better for a man to receive the value of his wages for his work rather than to receive a part of that value indirectly through house rent. But we may be glad that through one means or another the rents are kept down.

Building stone is so easily available in Ireland, and lime is found so near the surface in many counties, that with a little help the average Irish-man may enlarge his home if he is disposed to do so.

It is a curious fact, noted throughout the ages, that after a great war there follows a great building era. This is not because there are more people to house, but because people wish to live better. As Ireland was not very heavily engaged, so far as the Free State is concerned, in the late great war, one does not see there the active building that is so common in Britain. We believe, however, that as soon as the Free State gets past the burden of riot reparations, an era of very general cottage improvement will set in.

The basal idea of a beautiful cottage is furnished in the present farmhouse. It needs little, but it needs something, to make it perfect. The first step is to implant in the person who dwells in a house an ideal of a better house, and from that implanting everything will follow. Even now the idea of rose decoration has spread through entire communities until five or six farms in succession will be beautified in this way. Planning is more important than doing, because the plan, once it is rooted in a cottager's mind, will grow into accomplishment. Many an Irishman would be astonished to know that his little homestead is seen through these simple pictures in thousands of American homes.

An important improvement can be made by multiplying wells or piping water. Many a woman did we meet with her donkey cart, drawing water from a half mile or more. If water were valued according to a fair wage cost in procuring it, the price would be prohibitive. In fact it is so, because a housewife must, if she carries water, leave undone many things that would contribute to the profit of the homestead. No satisfactory civilization can be maintained unless all modern improvements are made. If one region has such improvements another region must follow or suffer from the handicap. Well-drilling on a large scale, as a community matter, is relatively a small expense.

The carts of Ireland are heavy out of all proportion to the animals that draw them. Perhaps their weight is an ancient hold-over from the time when no roads existed. The man power of Ireland is not now helped as it should be by modern devices. There are instances where farmers have combined in the purchase of machinery. The process ought to continue because it is the only possible method of progress where the farms are small.

The creameries of Ireland should be multiplied, for nothing else whatever contributes so quickly and profitably to the improvement of the land.

The day is long past, in Ireland or elsewhere, when villagers should be compelled to go to a town pump for water, or a farmer should be reduced to spading instead of plowing his field. Grain is a crop of too small yield to raise in a teeming country, near a market. Ireland ought to be able to supply England with potatoes and other produce and with more coöperation in farming, will do so.

The Irish farmer looks quizzically at one who makes such statements, and expresses a wish to know where the money is to come from, for such improvements. Some of it is coming from America, more will come.

It will come from some quarter when the Irishman wants money for this purpose more than he wants it for some other purpose. Agricultural fairs are held about Ireland. It is true more money is lost at them in horse racing than is made through increased knowledge and stimulated husbandry. But the Irish are becoming more alert to their proper interests. The political question has for so many years overshadowed everything else that there has been no time to think of what really ought to be done at home. The discouragement and heartache of generations is passing away. The Irishman must now save himself with the moral and sometimes the financial aid of America. These are the sentiments not only of an American like the writer, but voiced in all the large papers of Ireland.

The beauty as well as the use of Ireland must arise from its own people, and I fully believe they will show a new enterprise arising out of a new hope, in making Ireland more than ever a beautiful land.

UNDER THE BEECH — COUNTY CORK

SKY ARCHES — COUNTY KERRY

KILLYLEIGH — COUNTY DOWN

NEWRY WATERS — COUNTY DOWN

THE FAR BEYOND — COUNTY DOWN

BORDERS OF THE SUIR—COUNTY WATERFORD

A MOUNTAINEER'S COTTAGE—COUNTY KILDARE

SHORE OF UPPER LAKE—COUNTY KERRY

DOWN THE VILLAGE—COUNTY GALWAY

THE SILENCE OF THE HILLS—COUNTY KERRY

TOURING IN ULSTER

I F ONE lands at Larne from Scotland, he may make the run by the shore to Belfast, and thence begin the tour over the same route as one landing at Belfast. Steamers reach Belfast from Liverpool and other points. Should one come by motor from the Free State, one can, on the same journey, finish his sight-seeing by the shore route from Dublin, through Drogheda, and Dundalk.

Beginning then from Belfast, County Down would first appeal to us. As the season is always advancing and running away with one in Ireland, it is the natural thing to work from the south north, with the year. There is, however, less difference between the South and North of Ireland than one would suppose. The vegetation is practically the same, as the whole island lies in the influence of the Gulf Stream and the warm airs that accompany it. We were told by a Belfast man that there has been skating but one year in the last fourteen, in Ulster. The climate, therefore, is a little cooler than in the south, but it does not vary greatly. There would never be skating in the south, at least near the shore.

Following the shore from Belfast to Bangor, one sees at the north Belfast Lough. Bangor is a shore resort city, the headquarters for yachting and yacht-racing. It has, however, an ancient and interesting life of its own. According to the time at one's disposal, the peninsula to the east of Strangford Lough may or may not be investigated. There is a shore road against the ocean and another shore road bordering the lough, so that one goes and returns by different routes. Whether making this journey or coming directly from Bangor, Newtownards is reached. If Belfast is used as a headquarters, there is a direct road from this town into Belfast. Otherwise we drive southward from Newtownards through Cumber, to Saintfield, and Downpatrick. Here is a cathedral founded by St. Patrick. Its quaint early type (page 99) is well worth study. In this picture appears one of the ancient crosses, concerning which we have written.

A celebrated drive from Downpatrick proceeds through Castlewellan, and follows the shore, having the Irish Sea on the left and the Mourne Mountains on the right. The loftiest of these, Slieve Donard, rises about twenty-eight hundred feet, almost over our heads. The drive is a good introduction to the wonderful shore routes of Ulster. All the way from Newcastle, where the finer views begin, to Newry, at the north end of Newry Canal, there is a succession of splendors. After leaving the coast at Kilkeel, we bear westerly to Carlingford Lough. Here we have mountains on the right, as before, and looking across the beautiful lough, like a fiord, we have another mass of mountain on the southwest. Rostrevor is a delightful little city in the quaintness of its architecture and in its accessibility to different sorts of scenery. Two subordinate roads lead from Rostrevor directly into the Mourne Mountains, to Hilltown. Then there is the shore route on which we were following. Newry Canal is a natural body, but its appearance is so like a canal that the name naturally applies to it. One would do well, if time served, to pass down the western shore of Newry Canal from the town of that name to Carlingford, and thence back to Newry, leaving Dundalk somewhat on the left. The Mourne Mountains are so delightful that we find it hard to leave them, and return for one exploring trip after another about their bases. Returning from Newry, we run into Belfast through Banbridge.

A journey through Armagh should not be omitted. Leaving Belfast, we follow the same route on which we entered, as far as Lisburn. There we fork to the right for Portadown, and the ancient city of Armagh. It is full of rambling streets, up and down, and in and out. The great cathedral here is an effort to express, on the part of the Catholics of Ireland, their love and faith. The site is remarkably fine, perhaps not surpassed, if equalled, by that of any other cathedral. The long series of steps is vastly impressive. Here, as it is perhaps unnecessary to say, is the seat of the primate of Ireland. The location of a see is always an enlightening commentary on the early history of a country. It proves in this case that Dublin was not, in the early times, as important relatively as it is today.   Armagh is in the midst of a very rich region.   The second lowland plain in size in Ireland extends east, west, and north of it, and includes Lough Neagh.   The drive from Armagh to Monaghan leads one across the line into the Free State.   Incidentally, this is the point at which we entered.   We had been exploring the beautiful rolling districts of Cavan and Monaghan counties.

In blossom time the drives about Armagh are redolent with the scent of the apple, and delightful with its pink and white hillsides.   Armagh is worth while being made a center for an extended visit.   If time serves, there are many attractive routes from this city through a beautiful country district to many of the most ancient and interesting abbeys and castles.

Leaving Armagh, one may make the circuit of Lough Neagh through Dungannon, Cookstown, Moneymore, Castle Dawson, and Randalstown, Antrim, and so to Belfast.   Or, if one desires to follow subordinate roads, he may approach Belfast through Crumlin on the east of Lough Neagh.

This great lough is only forty-eight feet above sea level, indicating that all the country about here is recent geologically.   The shores of the lake do not anywhere come into contact with mountain chains, nor do the trunk roads touch the lake except at Antrim and at one other point west of Randalstown.

The city of Belfast is very large.   Indeed, it claims preëminence in this respect over Dublin.   The contention, however, can be made good only by ruling out from Dublin extensive districts which, by an ancient division, are not yet included in the city corporation.   Belfast is essentially commercial, and those who wish to investigate shipbuilding or the linen industry will do so here.   There has been here also a very extensive experiment in municipal aid for building tenements, which are rented at a nominal sum.   The city is proud and teeming, but the aftermath of the great war has brought many features of socialism to the front.   It is not the province nor the spirit of this book to enter largely into such questions. It is sufficient to say that a more diversified manufacture would probably be the solution of the present difficulty.   Belfast has many noble public buildings. It is seeking to embody in its government and in its campaign of education the best of modern life on the industrial side.

The shore road from Belfast north through Carrickfergus passes first many fine suburban homes, and then the great castle with its grim keep, an ominous reminder of the hard old days. At Whitehead and Black Head, a little north of it, the shores are bold, rising quickly into cliffs. Island Magee, forming Larne Lough, has an interesting drive, purely rural. North from Whitehead, on the west shore of the lough, we reach Larne, a city of recent development as a port.

Perhaps the most celebrated route in Ireland, aside from that to the Killarney lakes, and to some minds rivaling it, is that from Larne north, following the east and north coasts of Antrim. We were favored with glorious days of pure sunshine on the way to Glenarm.

Of the highest importance here, in the study of beauty, is the route inland to Ballymena, and back, by a second and parallel road. The routes are not trunk lines, and if one does not care for threading country roads, this journey may not appeal to him. The little city of Glenarm, guarding the narrow valley and river of the same name, is attractive for a long or short stay. Following thence north, around Garron Point to Red Bay, and Cushendall, we reach a celebrated vale, superior, in its way, to any other in the region, and, in the minds of some, supreme in Ireland. Here again, going inland to Ballymena, or turning back from Parkmore station to Red Bay, we have the advantage of looking up and down the vales. Beginning at the falls of Glenariff, and continuing to the ocean, one sees a crescent-shaped vale of great magnificence. The tree decoration is perfect, and the farms that lie in the vale are under one's feet like an airplane landscape. This glen is only one of many that may be explored from the shore resorts on this coast. There are seven exquisitely beautiful valleys, whose lower ends reach the shore between Glenarm and Ballycastle.

From Ballycastle to Portrush we are following the north coast of Antrim, and a series of scenes which stand apart in their character and magnificence. They include various bold headlands and castles and the Giants'

THE KENMARE RIVER—COUNTY KERRY

A ROSE TREE GABLE—CO. DOWN

A KENMARE BROOK—CO. KERR

PURPLE AND GREEN

A ROAD IN GLENARIFF

SIR JOHN BERMINGHAM'S CASTLE—COUNTY GALWAY

MOSSY SLATE—COUNTY DONEGAL

CARRICK-ON-SUIR—COUNTY TIPPERARY

THE TEACHER'S GARDEN—COUNTY KERRY

SS AND TOWER—MONASTERBOYCE

MANTEL——CASTLE DONEGAL

A NARROW WAY—CO. ANTRIM

COOMHOTA RIVER—CO. CORK

DUNGORY CASTLE—COUNTY GALWAY

CONG ABBEY—COUNTY GALWAY

BALLINABAD CASTLE——COUNTY SLIGO

BETWEEN HILL AND TREE——COUNTY KERRY

DOMESTIC PEACE—CO. CORK   DESMOND CASTLE——LIMERICK

ANCIENT DANISH CHURCH—DUBLIN   UP FROM THE BROOK—CO. CORK

Causeway, as well as several beautiful beaches, called, on the east side of the Atlantic, sands. Those who love drives looking down from great heights into the sea will find their appetites sated on this shore.

The Giants' Causeway has come in the minds of many to be a symbol for this part of Ireland. It is no more beautiful, and perhaps not more interesting, than other places on this coast. We should say that some of the glens are more attractive. Nevertheless, the Causeway is a marvelous natural feature. It belongs in the same class with Niagara Falls in the sense that it has been so much pictured and talked of that it has lost its freshness to our minds.

One must walk a considerable distance to see all of the Causeway, and the heights beyond it. The region seems to have been protected from most of those offensive booths that skirt the approaches to famous resorts. One would suppose, however, that protective measures on the part of the state should still be taken. The fee now exacted could then be used to remove rather than to erect fences, and to police the shore.

Portrush is the fashionable resort for bathing or pretending to bathe. The beach under the cliffs has striking beauty. If one wishes to make a headquarters at Portrush, for touring, the location will be well chosen. There is a southerly route through the valley of the river Bann, past Coleraine, and skirting the canal to Kilrea. Thence one may go to Magher and so east to Randalstown, Antrim, and Ballymena, then by Ballymoney back to Portrush. The return route from Ballymena to Ballymoney is largely on higher ground. The rest of the route is mostly through the lowlands. On leaving Portrush finally, the next and the last important shore point of Ireland to be visited is Londonderry. This city with proud history stands apart in the sense that is it the only large town for many miles. A line of transatlantic steamers calls here on the way to and from Scotland. The city is of much importance in every way, socially, commercially, historically, and as a center for esthetic journeyings. If one is ambitious to reach the most northern point in Ireland, he should go from Londonderry by the west shore of Lough Foyle to Moville, thence to Culdaff, and Trawbreaga Bay.

Malinhead is far and away the most northern outpost of Ireland. Returning on the same route as far as Malin, one goes to Londonderry by the
westerly route, touching Lough Swilly for a part of the way. This journey
is to be commended very highly, both on account of its intrinsic beauty and
the interesting rural developments. We count Londonderry as one of the
most important points in Ireland, from which to make delightful journeys.
Going southeast to Claudy, some ten miles, we came upon what proved to
be for us the most beautiful river scenes in Ireland. The magnificence of
the beeches, the paths by the bank, the waterside flowers, and every feature
required to compose an exquisite whole, was found here. One of these
vistas we named " A Bonny Dale " (page 55). At the close of a long
day, where nothing of a strikingly beautiful nature had revealed itself to
us, we reveled in this beauty. The sky was dull, but the air was positively
motionless. This absolute quiet is one of the rarest things in nature. We
observed another windless day in Ireland. Sometimes in America we
go a season through without being favored with this silence more than once.
We therefore recommend the Vale of Claudy as a solace for sad hearts.
It seems a little haven for which the soul has been longing. One may go
on past the Fore Glen to Dungiven and may return through Feeny, and
follow the opposite bank of the river back to Londonderry.

The River Foyle is like the Shannon in this, that it flows through
meadows and presents few high banks of pictorial interest. When one
leaves Londonderry finally, there is the choice of a route through the
north of Donegal, the route southwest, to the city of Donegal, the route
south through Strabane, Newtown Stewart, and the route southeast back to
Belfast. We journeyed through Newtown Stewart to Omagh and Enniskillen. This city is one of the most lively and industrious in Ireland. It
has both ancient and modern attractions, and lies on the borders of the
most remarkable lake, for the number of its islands and involuted banks.

If one wishes to follow through the lowlands to Newtown Butler and
Cavan, the journey forms an alternate route back into the Free State. If
we wish to avoid crossing the line, we may go from Enniskellen through
Fivemiletown, and so on east, through Belfast.

PARTICULARLY BEAUTIFUL PILGRIMAGES

THE Falls of the Liffey, on the southern route from Dublin to Water-ford, are so situated as to invite a day's excursion. The rapids of the river, seen by skirting along its banks for a half mile on the upper side of the bridge, are bordered by bold cliffs overhung on the one side with verdure. The numerous abrupt turns of the stream, the rocks covered with moss and lichens, the miniature falls, and the brilliance of the sun playing on the quiet stretches and on the white water, are long to be remembered. Coming down to the bridge itself, while the beauty of the scene has been too much obliterated by the semi-tropical luxuriance of vegetation, yet the climax of beauty is just above and just below the bridge. The overhang-ing trees are a great part of the composition, but they should be pruned out above, and particularly below, sufficiently to allow a finer view of the falls. One aspect of this we show on page 100. It was necessary, how-ever, to climb out on somewhat dangerous footing to procure the scene, as it should not be. One of the great assets of Ireland is its superb scenery, and it should not be made difficult for the public to enjoy it, as it is in this case. The densely shadowed walks here, under the hoary beeches, are most impressive. When the stream is running full, the effect is much finer. The pointed arch of the bridge, with its outworks, is a perfect crown to the composition.

The Liffey, in fact, throughout its course, is well worth viewing. At Leixlip, above and below the bridge, but particularly above it, the compo-sition satisfies our feeling for an old world river, a stone arched bridge, and quaint slated roofs.

Following the Grand Canal from Dublin, or rather planning to cross it occasionally, as one may near Naas, Newbridge, Kildare, and elsewhere, the scenes remind one of Holland. They are the more cheering and human since the canal is still in use to some extent, and the past generation is brought back by seeing the horses on the towpath. This canal was once the great hope of Ireland. It is startling to consider how rapidly methods change in these days. In about a century, we have passed from wallowing or being mired in the mud on through roads, and have reached the point where we may fly over them. Thus here in Ireland, there is the bridle path, the highway, the canal, the railroad, and the airplane soaring over all.

There is a valley in the Wicklow mountains, at their northern end, which takes one immediately from the great city of Dublin to the quiet upper air. It is called Glencullen, and is reached from Bray. There is another delightful tour from Bray past the Glencree Reformatory and Mount Venus. A third route from Bray follows the Scalp back to Dublin. A fourth is the most direct route, and the fifth is by way of Dalkey and Kingstown. The region about Dublin may be counted as a miniature Ireland, since it has its fine shore routes, and the remote and little frequented roads of its mountains. There are then the rich, intensively-farmed lands directly to the west through Maynooth. Here, indeed, may be seen in the ancient castle and the adjacent college, the old and the new. Maynooth is a celebrated educational center, in the very heart of the finest meadow country imaginable. This again is the route on which the Royal Canal stretches away, at an angle somewhat north of the Grand Canal. One interesting day was occupied passing from Dublin to Blessington, and Stratford, and Baltinglass. There is a wealth of fine upland outlooks on this route. From the last mentioned town we pass to Carlow, thence northward on the Barrow, an entrancing river, to Athy, and so back by Kilcullen to Naas and Dublin.

The hill farms of Ireland, whose cottages look for many miles along a valley, with its silver stream, and whose backs are protected by the mountains rising behind, are snug and much-to-be-desired nooks. Their residents are the lords of their region. Their sense of ownership is enhanced by their location.

The journey from Dublin to Trim discloses, on the river Boyne, calm, large scenes reminding one of the English fen country. At Trim, the most extensive abbey and castle ruins are found, and the castle is picturesque to

GWEEDORE—COUNTY DONEGAL

THE MOURNE MOUNTAINS—COUNTY DOWN

DOWNHILL GATES—COUNTY DERRY

SEAWARD FROM GIANTS' CAUSEWAY — COUNTY ANTRIM

THE BOX PATH — COUNTY KERRY

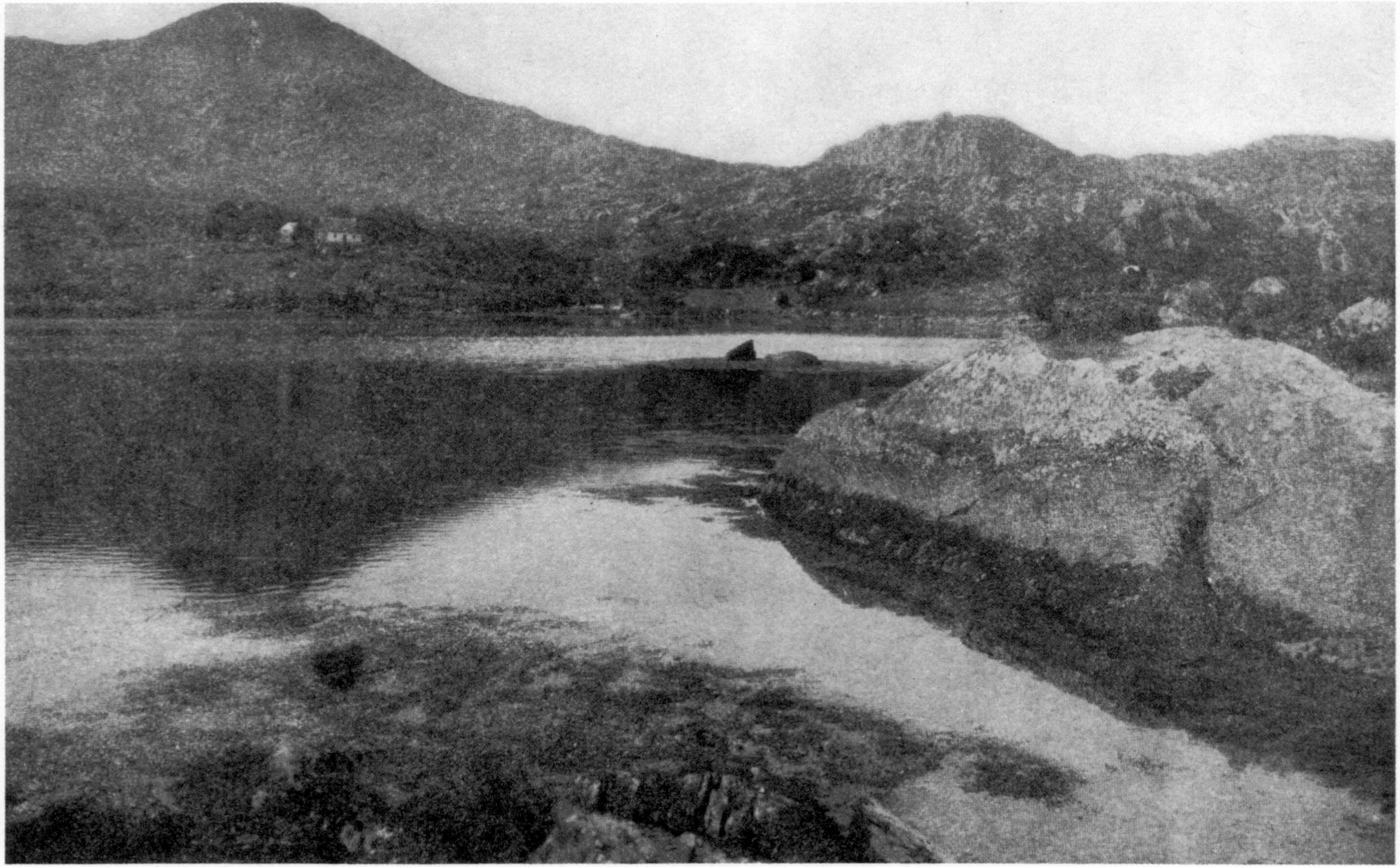

THE REFLECTED COTTAGE—COUNTY KERRY

the last degree. If one returns by the way of Navan and the hill of Slane, the day will have been spent among the most inspiring relics of the old times. The abbey on the hill of Slane has an outlook of unparalleled beauty, when the width of the meadow lands, with their rich farms, is considered. We are here on the historic Boyne, which gave the name to the most important battle ever fought in Ireland. The road from Slane to Drogheda, if one cares to take the shore route back, may include the site of the Battle of the Boyne. Our excursion from Drogheda to Monasterboice was one of the most memorable. Here is a little vale set apart, like a world alone. A very extensive ruin, the little chapel on the hill, the flowers in the crannied wall, and the quiet that reigns over all by the ancient foundation, were all profoundly impressive.

THE TIME TO SEE IRELAND

NOW is the time to see Ireland. Ireland needs you now, and will welcome you now with the greatest heartiness. The Irish do not feel sufficient unto themselves, in the sense that they lack capital, and sometimes courage, of the sort that will urge them to undertake important matters. They are trying to keep up their roads. The highways are largely without signs, but we can wait for such things. We estimated on one day's journey that it required at least twice as long to cover the ground on account of the numerous inquiries we were obliged to make. This would not be true on a main road.

But the word should be spread far and wide over America that the hotels are good enough and frequent enough. In the most remote parts of Ireland we would say that the hotels are rather better and more frequent than in the more highly cultivated portions. Of course this arises from the circumstance that in the remoter parts hotels are erected especially for tourists. There is absolutely nothing to hinder a delightful and extensive and long-continued journey through Ireland. If one dresses as we do for spring weather, he will almost never be too warm nor too cold. In the summer, the days are so very long that one can look until weariness ensues. Our health was good, although we often made a fifteen hour day.

Americans should get thoroughly in their minds what they are to expect in Ireland. There will not be in every small town a satisfactory hotel. Restaurants are practically unknown, outside of Dublin, Cork, and Belfast. One goes to a hotel for a meal, and unless it is a city hotel, he must wait long for the midday meal. All these are minor matters, and very slight matters. It is a constant marvel for the traveler that the roads can be so good. It is a still greater marvel that the food prices are so moderate. And as to rooms, one is sometimes almost ashamed not to pay more than is asked. Of course, the room is without bath, and as a rule, there is not even running water. The exceptions to these statements apply to the largest cities or to the very highest class of resorts only, and seldom in such cases. There is not a hotel in Britain, not to say Ireland, which we should in America call modern. The thing in danger of being overlooked is that practically the same conditions obtain in Ireland as in Britain. There is no good guide book of Ireland, but there will be, as several are preparing. At present one would perhaps best follow the various pamphlets issued by the railroads. All these lacks simply bring us more fully in contact with the people. We must ask more questions, and acquaintance is always interesting, and sometimes delightful.

Of another important matter we should warn the traveler. Do not fall into a rut, taking merely the say-so of others in relation to the beauties of Ireland. Nine-tenths of the pictures which we obtained were of regions never mentioned in any guide book. In fact, the particular scenes that we show are new to the public, as to their viewpoint, in every case. Instance the view on page 90. In what volume or what art gallery have you ever seen it? The same is true of the picture on page 87. We see an abundant number of pictures in the Vale of Ovoca. Who ever saw that on page 75? Yet is it not worth while? We have been through every one of the ancient guide books. For the most part they show street scenes, the backgrounds of which are the more notable but thoroughly conventional

buildings. There is not an Irish cottage in one of them. Whoever saw the
picture at the bottom of page 67, or that on page 57? These are the real
beauties of Ireland, and they are not found from any mountain summit,
or on any beaten track. Why should we not seek for such scenes as " A
Hawthorn Bridge " on page 23? Already very many persons have pro-
nounced it one of the most attractive small landscapes of Ireland. Any one
would know that " A Little Bay," on page 15, is a copy of an oil painting.
Only the fact is, that no one has ever thought it worth while before!

Hence my contention that if the traveler will look at the near things,
there is plenty of beauty. " Under Croaghpatrick," on page 134, contains
every element of romance, domesticity, and beauty. The mountain with
its dreamy and holy memories, the cottage home life, the river with its
broken stream, and the bridge, the mark of the movement of men, are all
here. Why not enjoy a tour in Ireland by finding scenes like these, rather
than to go hurtling through space to reach some trite and inferior view?
In a certain sense, it is a grave misfortune for a celebrated man to call attention to one particular portion of a country. We have in mind a town in
the White Mountains of New Hampshire, from which very little can be
seen, and where the street is on a humdrum level. Yet, because a person
of international reputation used often to visit there, it is imagined that there
must be some high merit connected with the town. A quiet little scene like
"Peace in Ireland " (page 227) is more thoroughly satisfactory than
anything notable of which we have heard. Nor let the reader suppose that
I am speaking from my own conceit. I am simply voicing the judgment
of others.

So visit Ireland now, and learn to love its soft repose. Look at the
mountains, not from them. Any stream is more beautiful if you dare to
put your bare feet in it, and see the shiners, or whatever the tiny creatures
are in Ireland, play about you. Get down, but look up. Peep behind the
fuchsias that grow eight or ten feet high, lining the hedges. Pluck the
foxglove which grows by millions, on lofty stalks, up into one's very face.
Nobody will object — flowers are free in Ireland. I never half saw the

beauty of moss until I sat on the rocks beside the streams of the mountain dells. The blossoms of the moss, in endless variety, stood up above it like creatures from another world. The rhododendron blooms skirt the streams and the edges of the woods. The floss silky, white peat flower covers over the bareness left by the diggers. The clover is observed by its odor, from the motor-car on a warm day. A miniature orchid fills the grasses. The lupin, to an immense height, occurs everywhere in gardens, not distinguishable at a distance from the larkspur. When all these decorations fill the valley, accompanied by the most luscious green, making good its place wherever it is permitted to thrive, and cloud and mountain fill the distance, when the people are gracious and their eyes shine with welcome, when the air is gentle, and especially when the roads are free from our hurried traffic, what could be better than a journey in Ireland?

We heard of collisions between the Orangemen and the Fenians in Glasgow and America. There was no such conflict in Ireland. A company of over ten thousand Orangemen had a day's outing in the Free State, amid the most complete calm. The speaker, an Orangeman, declared himself encouraged by conditions. Although he did not by any means agree with the government, he considered that it was doing the best it could, and was determined to administer the country justly.

Everywhere demands will be met, and if Americans turn aside to Ireland, they will not only remember their stay in that island as the most delightful episode in a transatlantic journey, but the people of Ireland will prepare for them. Every one who follows will find conditions better and better.

AN ORANGEMEN'S PARADE

WE WERE fortunate, or unfortunate, in being caught at Belfast on the day of the Orangemen's parade. There was deep significance in the occasion and not a little humor. All day long, twice over the ground, and a good deal of ground at that, followed the indefatigable marchers.

There were more big bass drums than I supposed were to be found in the entire island. There were drum and fife corps. There were banners, held by two perspiring men, with two enthusiastic boys on the guide ropes of every one. And what banners! Rich with silk, blazoned with bold and brilliant painting, huge as a ship's sail, they followed one another hour after hour, hundreds of them, up one street and down another. Then the bagpipers! If you happen to think of any kind of music that ever was in a parade, it was there. The fellows with the big bass drums had no assistance, as they do with us, where a small boy delights to go on ahead. The consequence was that the drummer was bent back like a bow, and the drum stood out before him like Spain on the map of Europe. And how they whanged and banged and tanged! And what a roar! We could but laugh to see one huge bass drum, as big as a hogshead, go by with the drum head split from side to side. The heroic drummer was determined to get out of it whatever was in it. A great many of the organizations in the parade were temperance societies. Whether they had anything to do with the Orangemen I am not clear. I was laboring under the impression that all North Ireland was in this parade. I believe it was claimed that forty thousand marched. But when we at length escaped from the city and reached Glenarm, there was another great parade. This day occurred on Monday. Saturday was an off day, it being summer everywhere. Tuesday was required to recover, so that the shops were not open from Friday to Wednesday. There was no fresh bread to be had during all that time. Since the war, the bakers have given up night work, and in order to have fresh bread, you must eat your breakfast at night, and your supper in the morning. Never mind. I have always contended that stale bread was better.

The Orangemen's societies have been especially active of late years, of course, owing to the insistence of northern Ireland that it shall remain a part of the British Empire. We tread here on delicate ground, and can easily plead that we know too little to form a judgment. But there is one fact which stands out like Glenluce Castle. Under whichever government anybody lives, the taxes are killing. North, south, east, or west, the burden in Ireland is awful. Let not any one cross the Channel to the shore of Britain, thinking to escape. Throughout Britain there is a kind of moribund condition in all trade, little and big, because it cannot bear the terrible burden.

People are willing to pay high for their right of self-government. The war simply means that we would rather be poor and free than to be rich and be slaves. We believe, however, that the bitterness of parties and societies in Ireland will be very much ameliorated if once the boundary lines are definitely settled. Then there will be no bone of contention left. On both sides of the line there is a kind of punctilious pride in seeing that justice is done to the minority. There are exceptions, and some big exceptions, but this is a book on beauty.

GLENLUCE CASTLE

ON a high and broad cliff, almost surrounded by the lapping waves, which in time of storm lash with impetuous fury the devoted rock, stands Glenluce Castle. Protected on the land side in the ancient day by a series of walls, it needs no other protection. Its bastions and towers rise numerously like high stalks in a garden. The soft turf comes to the very walls, and has even gone within and seized upon the court. In what distant age was there not some fortification at this point? As early as the time when men first combined to rob or to fend off robbers, there was doubtless a defensive work here. It looms grandly from the sea, and landward gives an impression that he must pay dearly who would cross its barrier armed. The old castle as it stands is the embodiment of feudalism. It has passed through tedious sieges when hunger made hollow eyes. More than one leader has become celebrated by his stubborn defence. The Walter Scott of Ireland is still awaited, to make this castle the scene of a romance to be known the world around. There is much patient learning in Ireland, and not a few brilliant men with a vocabulary and an imagination equal to the task. We think, however, that in Ireland the forward look claims most such men. They are willing to allow this famous old ruin to mellow with time and wear away in the blast of the Atlantic. They doubtless feel that the feeding of sheep about the walls is a finer emblem than the marching of mailed knights could be. It is only necessary to pause for an hour on this picturesque and historic spot to see what a distance men have traveled since the Middle Ages. With the same passions and capacities, men's hopes and aims are quite different. They long now to see a sanitary and dignified cottage for every family. They long to train all their children in the knowledge of letters. They wish to teach them to live outside of walls rather than within. The spirit of our age is imparting knowledge and inspiration, and affording the protection of a benign government in the remote places of the land as well as under castle walls. Our problems of education, of transportation, of defence, are as different from those of four hundred years ago as one may conceive.

Possibly the fundamental difference lies in this: that now the chief concern is to open for all an avenue of growth for the mind. Men need to be protected and encouraged in their thinking. It isn't a wall behind which we wish to shut up human thought. We are trying to emancipate thought. If the old knight with a landed estate, after early training, eternal vigilance, steadfast valor, could put off his armor at last, feeling that he had kept what came to him, he supposed himself to have done well. In the modern and better view, an enriched mind is the prime purpose for which the defensive powers of the nation exist. It is almost as if the urging purpose upward had led men to try every sort of government and every kind of society to find that best adapted for a full development of the man. We have not arrived at that society which can guarantee this opportunity of achievement. Some would say that it is as difficult to obtain an enriched mind as it was in the olden times. A student, however, of human achievement, will at once observe that those races that have brought forth the greatest number of enriched minds are not races who have lived where life is easy. We do not regard it as essential, or even as a possibility, that the best human enrichment should come easily. After the old castle wall was broken down, there was an obstacle in the man himself. Walls have never kept men from progress, nor have they enabled man to progress. The great business of the state is to stimulate advancement in its young citizens. The state that can inspire its youth is a good state. The experiments will go forward. We are not near the goal.

Nothing is more certain than that all political schemes and philosophies will fail. They ought to fail. None of them are sufficiently broad and deep and inclusive. Their failure is a step in progress. If you can induce a steamship owner, nay, if you can compel him to take out his old boiler that is likely to blow up, and install a new boiler, you have benefited him, although he cannot see it in that light.

Most of the work that men do consists in clearing away failures. But it is a necessary work. It is true in Ireland at the present time. Mistakes have been made there in all ages, and particularly in the history of the last few hundred years. Of course they were all stupid mistakes, but self-ishness induces men to take one-sided views, and to fail to see a subject intelligently.

We welcome all experiments. By that we do not mean that we would try anything once, a saying as thoroughly silly and unthinking as anything could be. The trying of suicide once, or the suicide of one's soul, is neither a mark of enterprse nor intelligence. But we will try anything once that men have not tried, and we will try anything that has come near approaching success. We will try anything that is based on the purpose of making the citizen bigger. For this, we need no castles, and, if the truth were known, we need few public buildings and no Grand Union railway stations. We need the alleys cleaned and the cottages improved. People have always begun at the wrong end with their improvements. God begins at the bottom. He brings up the white flower from the black soil. If we are engaged on stimulating the hindmost man, the man who is at the top will take care of himself. He always has gone marching on, but he has been too lonesome!

PEACE IN IRELAND—GLENGARIFF

AN IRISH HOMESTEAD—COUNTY DOWN

BEECH GLADE—COUNTY CORK

A DUNLOE CASTLE BROOK—COUNTY KERRY

MUCKROSS LAKE—COUNTY KERRY

A STONE PORCH—COUNTY DONEGAL

A LITTLE WALLED GARDEN—COUNTY SLIGO

IRELAND VIEWED FROM THE SEA

THE most wonderful way of seeing Ireland would be by sailing around it. A yacht, with power or sail, which could enter all the harbors, and weather all the headlands, would be a vehicle superior almost to an airplane. Landings could be made at all interesting harbors. Without the necessity of reaching a hotel at a certain hour, the dainty stillness of the morning and the beauty of the afterglow could be enjoyed. The best scenery is that which is looked on before breakfast or after dinner. The lover of sailing would find his paradise in such a journey. It may be that the journey has been made, but we do not see its results in pictures. One ought to start late in May, when the June brightness is about coming on, and it would perhaps be safe to continue the journey through July, certainly into July. The suggestion here made was brought to my mind by seeing the wonderful coast of Ireland around Queenstown. If I could also have sailed along Achill Island, and about Holy Isle, and the headlands of Antrim, if I could have gone bounding into Bantry Bay or Baltimore, if I could have approached the wonderful old sea route that leads up to Galway, what a delight it would have been!

PASTORAL IRELAND

IN THE earliest days of which we know anything in Ireland, the wealth was almost always in cattle. In this respect Ireland follows all human history. In Bible times property was synonymous with the herd. Our word " pecuniary," meaning " derived from the flock," shows the predominance in Roman and the early British time of sheep and cattle. It was ever so, from the beginning. The greatest law-giver was a shepherd. The first items of Irish history regarded the protection or the raiding of the flocks and the herds, and the castles were erected for their protection. When we speak of a grazing country, we really mean that the country is too rough or poor for anything else than grazing. By as much as land becomes highly cultivated, by so much the raising of cattle is pushed on into the mountains or the moors. In the ancient time, when there was very little intensive cultivation, the herds of Ireland were relatively far more important than they are to-day. Many place names indicate this fact. If all the names relating to watering places, folds, fortresses, pastures, and all terms relating to flocks and herds were taken out of the Irish language, a very large hiatus would be made.

The sheep of Ireland are an important element in the beautiful aspect of the country. We wonder if any one has ever written a disquisition upon the marvelous adaptability of sheep. They thrive in Egypt, where no rain ever falls, and the heat is intense; they thrive in sub-arctic countries. In Ireland, where, especially on the west coast, there is much rain, they have been a large element in the farmers' life. At the first thought, one would say sheep would not thrive in a wet or a hot climate. We have known but one instance in which over much rain injured sheep. That came to our attention in the spring of this year, in the British Isles, where it was necessary to gather the sheep in to attempt to get them dry. Undoubtedly the oily secretion preserves the wool from getting wet, more particularly in a country where much rain occurs. In some of the mountain roads we find sheep in the highway. They love to lie on its smooth surface. In many instances, as we came about corners, the sheep would rush in every direction, and leap over the most dangerous places, so that we feared for their safety. We would find them in the tunnels of the highway between Glengariff and Kenmare. They would not seldom take their rest in places where it was impossible for them to escape quickly. As soon as we saw them, we always moved on gently, because the sight of a flock of sheep is very engaging. To see the lambs, some of them as large as their mothers, always keeping on the off side as they ran away, was highly amusing. The mothers were more adept and careful, and less hasty in their flight. Perhaps the lamb is the only animal at which it is a pleasure to look at every stage of its growth. Its very awkwardness when small is amusing. One can do almost anything to a sheep, if he proceeds with sufficient gentleness.

The famous lines about Mary and her lamb were founded on an incident the characters of which are known. Pet lambs about Irish cottages are not so common as goats, yet occasionally one sees lambs lying against the walls of dwellings, or eating about the door. It has been so arranged that sheep and goats dwell together in the same pasture like Jack Spratt and his wife. One eats what the other will not. The goats clear up the weeds and the lambs feed on the grass, and between them they make a thorough job of it. Any pasture where both are kept regularly soon gains a delightfully smooth turf, running over the edges of the rocks. Such a pasture is, of course, the only perfect place for a picnic luncheon. After a little, the lambs begin to hover about to know whether there may not be a tidbit for them.

The roadsides of Ireland are capable of sustaining many sheep and goats. The goat being the hardier animal, and the wiser in taking care of itself, has nearly supplanted the sheep by the roadside, except in the mountain regions.

We saw little of local home carding, spinning, and weaving. When hand work began to be supplanted by textile mills, and a short period of prosperity dawned on Ireland in the establishment of such mills, the hand processes were largely abandoned, and the persons who had worked by hand became workers in the mills, if their residence permitted. Now that the mills have been given up, the knowledge of handling wool has vanished from nearly all the homes. An occasional rough sheep-skin garment in the natural state may be worn by the men in winter.

The cattle of Ireland, in the rougher country, are often allowed to flourish for themselves the year through, being raised purely for the beef market. Naturally they do not reach the proportions or the plumpness of stall-fed cattle, yet the Kerry cows, at their best state, are shown in county and national fairs, and come home with blue ribbons. The high-bred Jersey and Holsteins are exceptional in Ireland. An occasional family will keep a high-bred cow, and of course they are found in certain fine herds, and grades are bred for dairy farms. One of the most important advances to be made in Irish agriculture is that of the improvement of dairy breeds, a process which is likely to go on with accelerating movement. Ireland is much nearer to Britain than is Denmark. If Ireland were as intensively cultivated, and as scientifically, it could easily drown the Danish importations into Britain. The preaching of diversified agriculture is being taken up by the newspapers.

There is no more pleasing picture, to the lover of rural life, than a herd of cattle on a river meadow amid the little daisies and buttercups. " A Pasture on the Lee," page 145, is an instance of the very accommodating nature of two white calves lying close to the wall, where we stood. We were interested to see cattle feeding on the stream growth, and wading, so that the surface of the water was at the height of the manger. The cruelly developed horns of the Scotch cattle are not seen in Ireland. One feels safe to wander about the pastures at will. In fact, if modern mankind were interested in pastoral scenes, it would be possible to procure any number of them; but this age has got away from familiarity with such scenes, and it is the exceptional person who has the love for them. As we drove about, we would often be leaving a town in the morning, or coming into a town in the evening, of a market-day. On such occasions the roads were alive for miles with sheep and cattle, so there was nothing for it but to come to a dead stop, while farmer after farmer passed with their marketable stock. The poor beasts had sometimes traveled far. On market-day in Galway, the sheep would lie in the street so weary that nothing could budge them. But when the little pig goes to market, he is usually given a ride in the cart.

The enlivening and stimulating effect of market-day has been referred to elsewhere. We have not, however, called attention to the remarkable diffusion of ideas that occurs at markets. They constitute a sort of all-the-year-round fair. The comparison of weights and ages and conditions of stock, such as is actually forced upon farmers at markets, is a stimulative

A LITTLE MOUNTAIN—COUNTY KERRY

BOYLE ABBEY INTERIOR—COUNTY ROSCOMMON

A BEECH BORDER—COUNTY CORK

A BAY OF GALWAY

ST. JOHN'S ABBEY—COUNTY MEATH

LUSH WATERS—COUNTY CORK

KENMARE PEAKS—COUNTY KERRY

HIDING BEHIND BEAUTY

THE LITTLE LOUGH

AN ARM OF LOUGH NEAGH

A TANGLED GARDEN—COUNTY KERRY

RAPHOE CASTLE—COUNTY DONEGAL

COTTAGES ON THE OLD SOD—COUNTY WICKLOW

CARRICKFERGUS CASTLE—COUNTY ANTRIM

WATER JOYS—GLENGARIFF, COUNTY CORK

KILLARNEY CURVES—COUNTY KERRY

education. On the same occasion the matter of quality in farm vegetables, and of styles and strength in vehicles and machinery, can but receive consideration, and little by little there is diffused over the whole of the state a knowledge of the better methods. There is no county without its fine farms. The alert and the diligent have seen what could be done, and have set the pace. These men are the real benefactors of Ireland, and now that the improvements they make will be their own, we shall see rapid progress.

IMPORTANT SCENES IN IRELAND

1. Dublin: university, museum, monuments, Phoenix Park
2. The Hill of Howth
3. Malahide
4. Swords
5. St. Doolagh
6. Mellifont Abbey
7. Battlefield of the Boyne
8. The Hill of Slane
9. Kells
10. Trim
11. The road, Dublin–Wicklow
12. The Dargle
13. Falls of the Liffey, on Dublin–Hollywood road
14. The Dublin Mountains.
15. The Vale of Ovoca (Avoca)
16. Waterford: confluence of three rivers
17. Ardmore.
18. Cork: the Shandon church, cathedral, etc.
19. Queenstown
20. Blarney Castle
21. Glanmire: village and stream

22. Kinsale harbor.
23. Drive: Youghal, Linsmore, Fermoy, Cork
24. Cork, Bandon, Skibbereen, Baltimore Bay
25. Bantry Bay
26. Glengariff and its vaies
27. Glengariff–Castletown road
28. Glengariff–Kenmare road
29. Kenmare–Castletown road
30. Kenmare, Parknasilla, Waterville, Valencia, Killorglin, Killarney
31. Kenmare–Killarney road
32. Upper lake
33. Middle lake and Muckross Abbey
34. Lower lake
35. Gap of Dunloe
36. Torc Cascade
37. Killarney, Castlemaine, Dingle, Tralee
38. Adare Abbey and Castle
39. Limerick
40. Killaloe and Lough Derg
41. Ennis road to Cliffs of Moher
42. Galway and Lough Corrib
43. Cong Abbey and the Holy Isle
44. Cottages on Tuam–Athenry–Galway road
45. Connemara, Clifden
46. Leenaun, Killary Harbor, Lough Kylemore
47. Croaghpatrick and Westport
48. Newport, Mallaranny
49. Achill Sound and Island and Head
50. Ballina-Sligo road, *via* the Ox Mountains
51. Lough Gill, the circuit
52. Loughs Arrow and Allen, Bundoran, and Lough Erne
53. Donegal, Inver Bay, Killybegs, Andara, Letterkenny, Rosapenna

54. Milford, Ramelton, Londonderry
55. The circuit of Inishowen peninsula
56. Portrush, *via* Claudy, and Coleraine
57. Portrush
58. Dunluce Castle
59. Giants' Causeway
60. Carrick-a-rede
61. Ballycastle and glens
62. Cushendun, Cushendall, and the vales
63. Red Bay and Glenariff
64. Glenarm and the vales
65. Shore road *via* Larne to Belfast
66. Antrim, castle, Lough Neagh
67. Belfast–Bangor
68. Downpatrick and cathedral, *via* Saintfield
69. Newcastle and Slieve Donard
70. Shore road, *via* Kilkeel, Carlingford Lough, to Newry
71. Newry, Carlingford, Dundalk
72. Armagh, cathedral and vicinity
73. Road, Armagh–Enniskillen
74. Upper Lough Erne
75. Cavan and Monaghan
76. Longford, Roscommon
77. Road, Cullamore–Maryborough–Carlow
78. Road, Carlow–New Ross
79. Road, New Ross–Kilkenny–Carrick-on-Suir
80. Road, Clonmel, Cahir, Cashel and its hill
81. Tipperary — a long way, but we arrive!

PLANNING AN IRISH TOUR

ONE reaches Ireland first *via* Fishguard to Rosslare; second, Holyhead to Dublin; third, Liverpool to Dublin; fourth, Stranraer to Larne; fifth, going to or returning from America, Scotch steamers call at Belfast or Londonderry; sixth, to or from America, English steamers call at Queenstown; seventh, Liverpool to Belfast. There are various other subordinate routes from English ports or from one Irish port to another.

The establishment of a purely Irish-American line is mooted, but if the city of Boston is not large enough to be a terminal for some of the steamers that run to it, and afterwards go on to New York, we would doubt whether a line running to Ireland only, from America, would find sufficient traffic. Of course a line of small steamers might do so.

The first consideration in planning a tour is to ask what one really wishes to see most. If it is a matter of visiting the most celebrated points, then a day in the environs of Dublin, a day's ride to Cork, a day in Cork, a day *via* Bantry Bay to Glengariff, a day at Glengariff, and a day at the Lakes of Killarney, may be all that one would care to do. Some of the resorts to the north are somewhat fashionable, as Bundoran, Mallaranny, Rosapenna, Portrush.

If, however, one is a student of the old life of Ireland, then a cottage, castle, and church tour, including the natural scenery that would be passed *en route*, should outline a very satisfactory journey, and leave a far more accurate and lasting impression of Ireland than a tour undertaken merely for the sake of " doing " it. It is, of course, a shame to our humanity that one person should do a thing merely because another does. We are persuaded, however, from long experience, that as one has wittily said, the difference between custom and law is, one is afraid to break a custom. It is perfectly certain that Ireland is the last country in the world to visit merely for the purpose of making the grand tour. Ireland is not filled with statuary or a great deal of magnificence in carved stone. It is more interesting for its people, its simple rural scenes, and its village life.

IN CENTRAL IRELAND

A DONEGAL STREAM

MELLIFONT ABBEY—COUNTY MEATH

PORTRUSH—COUNTY ANTRIM

THE LURE OF THE MOUNTAINS—COUNTY DOWN

CASTLE OF CLAREGALWAY—COUNTY GALWAY

PETE AND REPEAT—COUNTY GALWAY

BETWEEN STREAM AND FOREST—COUNTY CORK

For those persons who, with a broad catholicity of spirit, are interested in everything human, Ireland is capable of supplying abundant delights, as well as giving one an outdoor year of university training.

A few practical suggestions. If one has an American car, it is well to carry a few spare parts and to start out with tires in good condition. We journeyed a great many thousand miles in Ireland without being obliged to visit a repair shop or buy a tire. We are presuming that the American will take his car with him. If so, he may suffer annoying delays unless he is thoroughly equipped. Traveling with a very simple car, or with a foreign car, it is, even so, possible to get far enough away from supply houses to suffer annoyance. Of course all the larger cities, perhaps twenty of them, have well-equipped garages; but they are not equipped to take care of the wants of large American cars. As to the expense of journeying, we found the usual garage charge to be a shilling or one and sixpence, which is certainly very modest. Even the charge for supplies is scarcely more than in England.

In certain seasons it is important to reserve rooms in advance in the popular houses, but if traveling in the spring and fall it is not worth while. Ireland is too recently recovering from its woes to be teeming with visitors, except in the height of the season. It is always best, if possible, to arrange for a journey a little out of season. There is less travel on the roads and more room in the hotels. June is not only the best month for weather, but the long days are desirable. The next months in order of preference may be as follows: July, October, May, September, August. There is an effort just being put forth to set out the merits of Ireland as a winter resort. In the south and west one would find the winter climate very mild indeed, though of course rather rainy.

Unhappily, there are many who cannot choose the time of their tour. Multitudes of Irishmen who left home in their youth yearn to return for a visit. Many of them never tear themselves away from the district in which they were born, during their brief sojourn on returning to their early homes. Then there are a vast number of sons of Irish parents who wish to see the homeland of their race, but who are either too prosperous to absent themselves from America for a long time, or for the very opposite reason must make their stay brief. Even to such we would point out that the ocean tariff is lower in the spring and the fall than it is in the summer. Also, it is worth while to say that conditions of second and third cabin travel are very excellent. There is much competition in this business, and the quarters and the food are better than were the best thirty years ago. Persons of culture and of good financial condition often go second cabin, or in the one-class ships. I heard one man complaining that the firm which employed him would not permit him to travel second cabin, but he much preferred it. He said that the fellowship of the passengers was much pleasanter. If one desired to make the Irish journey at moderate expense, one could leave the steamer at Queenstown, buy a low-priced car, tour Ireland, resell the car, and embark at the same point. Of course, this is far less expensive than taking over any kind of car, unless the journey were to be for a long summer and a large car were required. It is best to take all one's belongings in the car. We went into only one dining room in Ireland where evening dress seemed to be general. Even there we saw persons of importance in business suits. One may therefore ignore any-thing of the sort, and take care merely to be provided with warm clothing. We do not mean that it is cold in the summer, but it is much cooler than in America, and as rooms in hotels are seldom heated, and never in the sum-mer, and as chilly or wet days are likely to occur, one feels more com-fortable in driving in something besides a light summer suit.

There is a good thing to be said for the Irish weather in summer — it is seldom bad all day long. It is always better to go on one's way hoping for clearing air. An overcast day is very comfortable for driving, and an occasional shower frees one from dust. Our own experience was an excep-tionally dry tour in the liquid sense of that word.

At hotels it often appears that by walking up two flights one saves some shillings on a room. We found that this condition continued even in hotels which had elevators. The landlords have not yet learned that

Americans are willing to pay more for the upper rooms. One is never met with enthusiasm at a hotel in the British Isles. The guest deals invariably with a woman at the office. He may come and go, even in a small house, perhaps, without ever seeing the proprietor. Possibly, indeed, there is none. By the European system, a hotel man seems to consider it beneath him to accept money directly. It must be done through a clerk. The old plan of jotting down everything is still maintained at hotels, except that the charge for lights and attendance has passed away with the war. One will do well to take at table what is set before him. Any effort to obtain a special service usually causes more friction than the effort is worth. Everywhere since the war, oatmeal has made its way, and it is universally offered as the first course for breakfast. The guest will then be brought tea unless he very explicitiy requires coffee. The coffee should be ordered not too early, or it will be that left over from the night before; and not too late, or it will have lost its savor. One of the unsolvable mysteries of European hotel practice is that the dining room is called the coffee room, though at some of the meals coffee is not served, and, for the most part, guests never call for it, or, what is worse, wish they had not. This condition is not at all peculiar to Ireland.

Sunday is a hard day for hearty people. An early dinner is served, and at night one must take pot luck. In a great city in Ireland, it was somewhat after eight before we could get hot water in our rooms in the morning. The maids come on duty at eight. Those who wish to leave their rooms by a quarter after eight must be Spartan enough to use cold water.

We found no one unpleasantly demanding in relation to fees. All took quietly what was offered and seemed satisfied. It is often difficult to leave a hotel in the morning. Even when the bill was asked for the night before, we were until half-past nine in the morning, in various instances, before we could get our reckoning.

The money denominations in Ireland are the same as in England. Express cheques are most convenient, and letters of credit are a great bore, because provincial banks require at least a half hour to compute a payment. Even so, they all have their own rates of discount.

These are all petty matters and worth no man's serious consideration, but to know beforehand is to avoid even minor annoyances. Parcel post directed outside of the country entails various humorous experiences. On one occasion I visited a post office five successive times before I succeeded in getting the matter arranged to the satisfaction of the authorities. On the first occasion I was told that I could not send more than four pounds to America by parcel post. On the second occasion I was told that it could not be registered. On the third occasion, that if registered, it must be sealed. I was obliged to journey two miles back to my hotel to borrow a taper and sealing wax. After two more obstacles had been overcome, my parcel, re-wrapped four times, was accepted. Yet the functionaries were always kind.

We did not find any corner in Ireland where English was not well understood. The children were better behaved than American children. They did not stand begging for rides. Every one cheerfully turned out of narrow roads.

Simplicity and kindness of manner on the part of the tourist will carry one through anywhere in Ireland. One should not go there if he feels above the people. In fact, there is no room anywhere in the world for a person of that sort. We never failed to arrive at a purposed destination, and never in Ireland used our motor lights. It often occurred to us, however, that a camping tour in Ireland, for those who like that sort of thing, would be very agreeable, for excellent sites could be found in every county, and supplies of milk, eggs, bread, chicken, ham, of any necessary thing beyond the course dinner, are easily had everywhere. In short, every one will carry away from Ireland a good impression in regard to most matters. The only thing is to remember that one is traveling in a country which, though naturally rich, has never been actually so, and which has recently passed through a transitionary period and is even now experimenting. So far as safety is concerned, there is nothing to ask more.

GETTING THE MOST OUT OF IRELAND

THERE are two ways of getting good out of a country. One way is by spending the revenue of the country elsewhere; the other is by having an appreciation for the country according to its merits. It is an old story, that we get from any subject in proportion as we bring an equipped mind to consider it. The geologist will get something from Ireland; the botanist, like the bee, obtains his honeyed information. The historian derives a different revenue from a country. The artist will take his quota. He will show us colors and forms that we did not see, although we were looking, or supposed we were looking. A poet or a social student may go over a country from which all the others have made their gleanings, and will nevertheless take from a country as much as if no one had preceded him. The sources of information, of inspiration, of beauty, of intrinsic wealth of every sort in every country, would seem to be almost inexhaustible. Thus a man who says he is not interested in a country advertises himself as out of touch with nature and art. It is nothing short of amazing how much that is good is unnoticed in every country.

If Ireland had been as thoroughly canvassed on the esthetic side as has Holland, the fame of Ireland would be spread in every land for its beauty. Yet Holland is not a country with anything like the natural attractions of most other lands. It is a standing example of how much can be gleaned from a country by prepared minds. The cultivation of the soil is the principal use of the country, according to the usual expectation. We venture to believe that it is a very secondary matter in comparison to cultivating the people. All men who have gone to Ireland have carried something away. Perhaps it was a carved souvenir pig. Perhaps it was the pleasing recollection of landscape.

In order that visitors to Ireland may be enriched as much as possible by their visits, I make bold to suggest the perusal of Joyce's *Antiquities of Ireland,* if it can be found in local American libraries. Unhappily the book is out of print. Of course, current histories of Ireland are available, and while there are no formal guide books, the investigating traveler perhaps gets on better without them, because he is not tempted to scan them instead of the scenery.

Some of the Irish newspapers are excellent, especially one published in Dublin. The editorials were of so fine and strong a quality as to leave a deep impression upon me. Furthermore, the writer was broad and sympathetic, and free from any particular fad or ism.

If one wants information in a rural community, a clergyman can often assist, and he invariably does so with pleasure. Clergymen are sometimes the only educated persons in rural parishes. Their eyes lighten to see a traveler, especially one from America. Furthermore, they are often the only persons who can tell where quaint or beautiful cottages may be found, or lovely curves of streams. For these most important things are never mentioned in print. In fact, there would seem to be a conspiracy of silence in regard to everything except the highest mountains and the biggest lakes.

This leads one to remark that we must find things for ourselves, not only in Ireland, but elsewhere. There is an occasional person who advertises for a wife, but the average sensible citizen finds one for himself. It is so with scenery. If we take the word of others as to what constitutes beauty, we lose all the joy of discovery. We degenerate into that class of itinerant imbeciles who go to a place so that they may say that they have been there. Ireland is very rich in interest for the seeker, but it is the last country in the world to visit for those who must have a guide.

I hope it is not superfluous to say that no understanding of Ireland can be had unless the viewpoints of its people are studied on the ground, together with their reasons for thinking as they do. The first great fact about men is that all men's views are somewhat warped. That statement includes ourselves. When we reach England, we find another opinion than our own. In Ireland there is still another opinion expressed. It is a marvelous circumstance that we agree in the main with our neighbors. Not that we lack political parties, and differences of opinion; but in the main Americans are for America, the English are for England, and the Irish are for Ireland.   Not only is this to be expected, but it ought not to be otherwise.   Men would be illogical unless they were moved by the considerations that govern their locality.   We can only say again, that had we been born in southern Ireland, we should agree with the people of that country.   In northern Ireland, our view would have been affected by our location.   The Irish people understand that.   We found a man who had lived forty years in Galway, who was diametrically opposed in practically all his opinions to his neighbors, because of a difference in training and ancestry, but who lived in perfect harmony with them, and was trusted and patronized to a great degree.

Reverting, however, to landscape beauty, we have noted in thousands of instances that people are most interested in that which they understand. Those who were reared in a plains country like it.   The love of other landscapes than those with which we are familiar argues some breadth of mind, at least.   One often hears travelers say, " This may be very fine, but give me old Iowa, or Massachusetts," as the case may be.   It is difficult to be impartial.   Perhaps, also, it is not always wise, nor desirable.   It may not always be creditable to our nature not to be prejudiced in favor of those whom we know best, and the scenes that we view oftenest.

A CONDENSED HISTORICAL OUTLINE

THE mythical and the legendary aspect of Ireland, like that of most countries, is perhaps more pleasing to read than the more solid facts that emerge later.

The very name, in Celtic, for Ireland, Inis-Fail, the Isle of Destiny, is most suggestive, we might almost say prophetic.   Another name, Inis-Ealga, Noble Island, shows the very early feeling of patriotism and appreciation for the singular merits of Ireland.   The name Fiordh-Inis, meaning a woody island, reminds us that once the forests were quite general.

The island was known to the Greeks and Romans. Plutarch gave it the name Ogygia, the ancient country. Here again is a suggestion that the region already had a history. There was in very ancient times a name still preserved, Eire, which in one form is Erin, and that has been taken as the usual poetic name.

The Romans first called it Hibernia, which name is also familiar to us, but at a subsequent period they called it Scotia. This name again has in it a whole volume of history. It calls to our mind the circumstance that Scotland got its name from the emigrants to Scotland from Ireland. It is thought that the name Ireland was adopted by the English, after the Norman conquest, from the ancient name Eire.

Who the ancient people were, racially, is still a mooted question. While they are by some evidence thought to have been dark and short, the name Formorian, by which they were called, refers in early Irish literature to giants. The first invasion of Ireland that seems at all historically established, was Belgic. These invaders were called Firbolgs. They were probably of a somewhat higher grade than the race they conquered. It is never safe to forget that a race is almost never exterminated. In England, the Britons, driven into Wales and Cornwall, were really supplanted. The Firbolgs, on the other hand, seem to have overrun, rather than to have exterminated. We then hear of the Danaans. They are thought to have been large, blond men, like the Norsemen, and were probably from Scandinavia. They were undoubtedly of the same race as those who came centuries after as Danes. There is even an invasion of a people called Milesians or Scoti, who were able to give their name to the land, though it was a name applied by foreigners rather than by the people of Ireland themselves.

The usual small tribal division of Ireland, such as we see in early England, prevailed. Those who are familiar with Scott's tales understand the intensely loyal and deeply ingrained clan spirit. In other countries this local loyalty has been outgrown, but it is only of late that the Irish people have merged fully in their feelings into a single loyalty. That is to say,

LOUGH GILL CLIFFS—COUNTY SLIGO

CARN CASTLE—COUNTY ANTRIM

OFF BANGOR

ABOVE THE LOUGH—COUNTY MAYO

A LITTLE BIRD'S HOME—COUNTY GALWAY

THE AMPHITHEATRE—GIANTS' CAUSEWAY

BARRIERS—COUNTY KERRY

BLARNEY CASTLE

KYLEMORE LOUGH—COUNTY GALWAY

they have been unified for the most part since the English domination. It is true that all Ireland was brought together under one king long before that time, but the clan loyalty did not blend wholly in national loyalty until after the English conquest.

The Christianizing of Ireland occurred very early, so that for three centuries it was perhaps pre-eminent in the world, for its religion and culture. Patricius was thoroughly Romanized, as his name may indicate. He was taken as a slave into Ireland by one of those raiding kings who made the piratical expeditions to the shores of Britain and France. He remained long enough in Ireland, by this amazing providence, to become fitted to return as a missionary. After he escaped, he was educated at Rome, and fulfilled his longing to become the apostle of Christ to Ireland. Then, as now, Ireland exercised a strange fascination over any one who visited it long enough to understand it. Patricius was a Celt, from Gaul, and probably understood the Irish character the better, although his equipment of course placed him far in advance of those to whom he preached. He was fired by a splendid passion for the salvation of Ireland, and he lived to see nearly the whole of the island accept Christianity. It is one of the vastest works ever achieved by one person. He arrived in Ireland about 432 A.D., and continued his work there for about sixty years. He did not confine his activity to preaching, but founded schools and superintended the erection of churches. With splendid zeal, he overthrew the pagan emblems so thoroughly that it is difficult to trace history before his time in Ireland. His name will be found in place names all over Ireland, connected with wells, churches, mountains, and every other natural feature. His life forms almost the noblest personal chapter in the history of Christianity since the time of the apostles. It is not to be wondered at that his name is still held in the highest reverence in Ireland. He stands supreme there as the father of the faith. We know enough about him to love him. He had obtained sufficient Roman culture to engraft their ideas of order and law upon the Irish people at least in their religious establishments.

But with his death, in the century following him, the Irish church, filled with a double portion of his spirit, became the nursery of missionaries to the parts of Europe not yet Christianized. The method was not one of force such as was at times used by Charlemagne. The Irish missionaries, like their great Prototype, and like Patrick, accomplished their labors by spiritual persuasion, and placed no dependence on the arm of flesh.

Great schools founded by the spiritual descendants of St. Patrick became the most illustrious in Europe. Their students came in great numbers, not only from Britain, but from the Continent. Ireland was thought of as a brilliant center of culture in the arts and sciences as well as the source of religious inspiration. Its missionaries penetrated Germany. They appeared at the English court of Alfred, and were well known by Charlemagne. They found the courage and had the enterprise even to preach in the Hebrides, and many of the scattered islands about Britain and Ireland. Many of these islands became the centers of religious foundations. Ireland itself was then denominated " The Island of the Saints." We are informed that the Irish received the students who came to them, and supplied them with all necessary things at the cost of the state, even to books and teachers. Great numbers of monasteries arose. From Armagh as a center, with its seven thousand students, schools which are said to have emulated it in spirit and equalled it in numbers arose at Clonmacnoise, Lismore, Bangor, and Mayo.

At this time the decline of art throughout the decadent Roman Empire was such that we should mistake by supposing that the classic period of Ireland was a great period in art in the same sense as the classic period in Greece. The particular point is that the torch of culture in Ireland was brighter than elsewhere at that period. The beautiful work done on vellum by the Irish monks, and their jeweled croziers, were the most remarkable that have come down to us, especially, in the latter example, the cross of Cong.

The Count de Montalembert in his work, " The Monks of the West," lays stress on the circumstance that Ireland was the only section of the world where the Gospel took possession without bloodshed.

This comparatively happy state was not to continue. The sea rovers, Vikings, representing the quintessence of heathenism, descended upon the devoted coasts of Ireland. Many of the great ecclesiastical foundations fell into their hands. They carried away the sacred vessels and used them in their drinking bouts; they tore off the jeweled missals and decorated their arms and armor with the spoils. They burned the sacred edifices and cut down the priests, and even the women, in capricious and useless slaughter. By the eleventh century, when Brian Borhoime gathered together the broken fragments of Ireland, the fine culture of the earlier age had dwindled away.

This condition was brought about by successive swarms, who made good their landing on the Irish coast. They are sometimes called Lochlanni, or people of Lakeland, meaning Norway. Others came from Jutland. Under the general term of Dane, history groups all these races. They seized upon Dublin, Waterford, Wexford. It is said that they especially loved Ireland because the contour of some of the estuaries reminded them of the fiords of their native land. This great conquering race, of the same breed as the Normans who, after consolidating Normandy, took England, has proved itself perhaps the mightiest force since the Romans. They did not by any means overcome all of Ireland. They established some subordinate kingdoms, as at Dublin, but, as happened in England, the old inhabitants at length became dominant over the invaders. We speak of course of the Danes, and not of the Normans proper. Nevertheless it is near the coast that most of their fortifying and governing was done, but on the coast they were dominant, and in addition to the cities we have named, made Cork and even Limerick centers of political and commercial power.

At length, before the millennial period, they accepted Christianity, although they seem to have done so quite generally through English influences.

The early kings of Tara, whose ruins have lately been mapped with great accuracy through the discovery of a descriptive manuscript, for a long time exercised overlordship in Ireland. By a variety of feudalism peculiar to Ireland the kings of Tara lorded it over the subordinate kings.

Brian Boru, in the year 1000, one of the most successful warrior princes of any age, became by conquest the over-king of Ireland. The Danes had made a compact with their brethren of Denmark, Scandinavia, and Scotland and the islands, and proceeded to carry out what they intended should be the total subjugation of Ireland. Brian was the national hero who met them in the year 1014 on Good Friday, at Clontarf, on the northern sickle of the Harbor of Dublin. There are said to have been a thousand men in armor and three thousand others on the Danish side, who lay dead on the field. But Brian mastered, in death. The slaughter on the side of the Irish was scarcely less. It was the end of the dream of complete Danish conquest.

In any fuller consideration of the history of Ireland, its main divisions, each containing several counties, follow, roughly, ancient kingdoms of Ireland, as Munster, etc. In each of the five grand divisions certain tribes predominated as in Ulster, the O'Rourkes, the O'Reillys, etc. The loyalty of the Irish for their particular section is very strong, even today. The family ancestor is traced back for many hundreds of years, perhaps for a thousand years. Unhappily, with this family pride, went the willingness to engage in conflict, such as marked the clans of Scotland. As the Greek states were obliged to unite against the Persians, so, according to McCarthy, the Irish coalesced against the Danes, while the Romans were still to come; that is to say, the Normans.

No sooner had the Normans fairly settled themselves in the saddle in England than some of their chieftains looked towards Ireland. It is said that William Rufus boasted that he would bridge St. George's Channel with a fleet of ships. But John of Salisbury obtained from the Pope, an Englishman, Adrian IV, a grant of a portion of Ireland, in 1154. The conquest proceeded, by historical analogy, with other conquests. The invaders sided with various ambitious chieftains, and set the people against one another. Richard Strongbow, Earl of Pembroke, became a great force

DOWN BY THE SHORE—COUNTY KERRY

THE SMOKE OF EVENING FIRES

A TYRONE RIVER

CROAGHPATRICK COTTAGES—COUNTY GALWAY

A BALTIMORE COVE   PINE ABOVE PALM

WHERE THE WORLD RESTS—COUNTY DONEGAL

JOYCE'S RIVER   A SWIMMING POOL ON THE LF

DIAPHANOUS LARKSPUR—COUNTY QUEEN

TIDE MARKS—COUNTY CORK   SEA SENTINELS—CO. ANTRIM

A PEAK IN DONEGAL

A VALLEY HOME—COUNTY ANTRIM

OLD MUCKROSS—COUNTY KERRY

A HIGHLAND VALE—COUNTY WICKLOW

BLACK AND WHITE HEADS—COUNTY ANTRIM

OVER THE HEDGE—COUNTY WICKLOW

MOUNTAIN AND LILY—KERRY

WATER GRASSES—CORK

KILLARY HARBOR—COUNTY GALWAY

in Ireland in spite of the orders of the English king that he remain at home. With this invasion begins the slaughter of the Irish people. The Norman-English began to settle on the conquered lands, and ever since, until the present age, a system of land tenure has obtained in Ireland, which was sufficient to render it always a poor and discouraged country. It is obvious that the most diligent man and the most ambitious will not improve his holdings for the exclusive benefit of his landlord. In spite of the difference in race, we believe that had the English land system been in vogue in Ireland, there would have arisen a great and rich yeoman and middle class to give Ireland that stability which the ownership of land invariably encourages.

However that may be, the English conquest was finally complete. The population was not driven away, but all the natives were treated as aliens. The legal disabilities were numerous and crushing. Hence there arose a permanent condition of alternate subjection and rebellion.

Now ensued a peculiar change. The Norman conquerors who settled on the land gradually got the Irish point of view. The English were constantly at variance with those of their own blood who had settled in Ireland. A statute forbade the use of the Irish language on the part of the English. Another forbade intermarriage with Irish families or the adoption of Irish customs. New colonists came in, and were gradually absorbed. But no remedy was ever found. We have said that the English conquest was complete, but to become so it was carried on through hundreds of years. After the Scotch had defeated the English so terribly at Bannockburn, the Irish thought they discerned hope in a new rebellion, and asked aid from Scotland. They even went so far as to offer the realm to Edward Bruce. He invaded Ireland and conquered in every fight. Yet after a little he was obliged to ask the help of his brother, King Robert, and he wasted his own men in hard bought victories. Robert, after some successes, was obliged to retire at length into Ulster in 1317, and soon after returned to Scotland. Edward, left alone, was finally defeated at Dundalk, October 5th, 1318, fighting against an army ten times the size of his own. He also met his death in this battle, closing one of the most brilliant, brave, but ill-judged attempts ever made in Ireland.

Under Edward III of England, was enacted the Statute of Kilkenny, which was especially evil in its effect upon Ireland. It resulted in a successful rebellion under the O'Neills, who gained ascendancy in Ulster while the DeBurgs attained the lordship of Connaught and united with the native Irish, and became themselves thoroughly Irish. Absentee landlordism had been recognized as a great evil in Ireland for hundreds of years, and though statutes were enacted against it, they were ineffective. The Statutes were intended to wipe out the Irish language and customs. They also prohibited intermarriage and foster nursing, but only embittered the quarrel.

The English pale denoted originally the four shires of Dublin, Kildare, Meath, and Louth. This strip, twenty by fifty miles, was in a certain degree English. The King's writ did not run effectively beyond this limit. The remainder of Ireland was parceled out between the chiefs originally Irish, and those who had become so, having settled from England.

Under Henry VIII, Sir Thomas Cromwell was employed to reconquer Ireland, and at length the will of the king became law over the whole island. A more just form of government was instituted, but the incoming of the Protestant revolution in England added the flame of religious difference and none of the Irish forsook their old faith. They were united as they never had been against the English. Space does not permit even a cursory record of the massacres, wars, plots, that followed for fifty years. The Geraldine League was at last a great and successful enterprise. In subsequent conflicts the Geraldines were, however, defeated, and the west of Ireland was laid waste until it was almost desert. The estates of the rebellious chieftains were confiscated and distributed among Irish nobles and gentleman adventurers. They, however, did not succeed in colonizing the island to any extent.

A new rising under Tyrone was overcome by Lord Mountjoy, at Kinsale, in 1601. This ended the conflict between the Tudors and the native Irish.

It was the opinion of Lord Bacon that until Ireland was thoroughly colonized by English farmers, there would never be rest in the land. Nearly the whole of Ulster was seized and the population driven out. These latter took to the mountains and bogs, and were hunted like beasts. The city of London settled Derry, henceforth called Londonderry. From this great and terrible injustice arose the settlement of Ulster. Under Charles I, certain concessions were granted to the Irish in the way of security of tenure, but promises of the king were broken, and Wentworth ruled with a stern hand. Hence rose the designation of "thorough." He increased the army, and made it a very efficient instrument. The validity of titles was again attacked and no man felt safe in his holdings. Wentworth, however, did encourage agriculture and navigation, and though he suppressed woolen manufacture, he assisted in the development of the linen industry, which really dates from him.

With the coming of Oliver Cromwell into power, there was concentrated rebellion and concentrated retaliation for the same. This is a story which the Irish and the English are trying to forget. It was estimated that twenty-five thousand Protestants were murdered. A massacre under Cromwell after the successful siege of Drogheda, it was claimed by him, was permitted in order to cow the Irish into submission. He is said not to have permitted the killing of unarmed men, but excepted the friars and priests from this rule. A massacre of the garrison of Wexford followed. As terrible as these things are, we in cold blood and at a distance presume that in the end they may have terminated the conquest sooner. It is sometimes forgotten that the garrison of Drogheda was largely English. The settlement of 1652 permitted the conquered army to leave Ireland and to serve in any foreign state at peace with the English government.

By this means many parts of Europe received respectable Irish contingents into their armies, and from this time on, for a hundred years, more or less, the enterprising and militant Irish were largely soldiers of fortune. Some of them reached a great place in France and Germany. They became leaders of armies. The Irish have formed a very large contingent of English armies, in India and all over the world. Owing to the oppressive laws against commerce and manufactures in Ireland, there was almost no other career open to the Irish. Had the bravery and the brains of the Irish people found an outlet at home, there is no reason to doubt that Ireland might have grown to a very great degree of wealth and culture.

The Cromwellian settlement made provision for the Adventurers. The term signifies those who undertook the re-settling of Ireland from England. Ireland was used, in parcels, to make good to the soldiers of the commonwealth their arrears of pay, or to settle debts due for commissary supplies to the army of the Commonwealth. Connaught was designated to be the reserve for the Irish people, and Protestants and English who desired to remove from Connaught were to receive equivalent estates in other parts of Ireland. This arrangement was intended as a virtual imprisonment of the Irish nation, because Connaught can be guarded against on the coast and the river Shannon. Of course, in the enforcement of the law, many exceptions, owing to age or for special reasons, were made.

At the Restoration, there arose hope for a general turning out of the settlers under Cromwell, and a reinstatement of the former owners. But after much dispute it was found that whatever settlement was made, hardship would be worked, and eventually the Adventurers surrendered a third of their allotment. Thus the settlers and the owners were hardly dealt with on both sides. The friends of the king who had helped him to return could not be satisfied, and the former adherents of the commonwealth shared their dissatisfaction.

With the coming in of James II he found that in the Irish Parliament the Episcopalians were the only hearty supporters of his cause. The Nonconformists were Whigs. James being a Roman Catholic determined so far as possible to favor the Catholics of Ireland but was somewhat unfortunate in the choice of his instrument, the Earl of Tyrconnel. He eventually disarmed all the Protestants except in the North of Ireland, and built up an army of twenty thousand men devoted to the Catholic interests.

FUSCHIA AND ROSE——COUNTY ANTRIM

LEDGES ON THE LEE——COUNTY CORK

CARRICK-A-REDE CLIFFS — ANTRIM   TWELVE PIN RANGE — GALWAY

CHECKERED FIELDS OF ANTRIM

KILLARNEY ISLANDS

KILLARNEY

THE CATHEDRAL—CO. ARMAGH   UNDER THE CREST—WICKLOW

A KERRY LOUGH

But when Lord Antrim came before Londonderry with twelve thousand men (though perhaps this force is far overestimated) the apprentice boys of Derry shut the gates of the city against him, and this act became the beginning of a powerful opposition to King James. In Enniskillen the Protestants also rallied. With the fall of James, the Protestant interests again triumphed. The defense of Londonderry is one of the most · stubborn and notable in history, and was made good against the Catholics. In 1688 Tyrconnel's men were driven back from the attack at Enniskillen. Followed many contests and the complete and bloody victory of the Enniskillen partisans, who had received help from William of Orange, lately landed.

The remainder of the history of Ireland is recent enough to be known in outline by most Americans. The French supporting the exiled English king supplied him with money, troops, and especially French officers, who organized an Irish army. James landed at Kinsale March 12, 1689, went to Dublin and summoned a Parliament. It is an amazing fact that so far had the English settlers become Irish in spirit that only about a quarter of this Parliament were Celts. Naturally this Parliament, called at such a time, indulged in unwise and extreme measures, so that in spite of its good legislation, the overthrow of King James' party at the Battle of the Boyne and in subsequent contests, threw matters back where they had been before. The Battle of the Boyne was bloody and fierce, and at one time of doubtful outcome. William, by his able lieutenant Schomberg, at length completed this last conquest of Ireland, with the help of Ginkel, another general of William, who advanced on Athlone. The place was obstinately defended as a forlorn hope by the Irish, and at last Ginkel conquered a ruin. St. Ruth, the French commander, with the Irish, was defeated at Aughrim, losing thousands of men, and the war was finally ended with the treaty of Limerick, in 1691. The English Parliament, however, failed to carry out the obligations under this treaty, and the king, bowing to policy, suffered its repudiation. The English Parliament was Protestant and prevailed over the mildness of William. The Catholics, who were four times the number of the Protestants, owned only about one eleventh part of the soil, and that the poorest part, after a fresh confiscation of over a million acres.

A settlement was made in 1695 depriving the Roman Catholics of means of education for their children, either at home or abroad. Another act deprived them of the right of bearing arms, or keeping a horse worth more than five pounds. Various other enactments of a nature to hinder the progress of the Irish followed, and the history of the next ten years is one of shame and, what is worse politically, failure to accomplish the result. The peasants for hundreds of years have felt that they were unjustly excluded from lands in which they ought to have a fee simple. Various organizations of White Boys, Oak Boys, Steel Boys, Peep of Day Boys, and so on, arose, to defend the Protestant interests, and the Catholic Defenders, another organization, overspread Ireland to defend the Irish Catholic interest and ended in the Insurrection of 1798. The dreary tale of conflict goes on. A Catholic Relief bill was passed in 1793. It removed the disabilities relating to property. It enabled Catholics to vote, and to keep arms in some cases, and to hold civil and military offices, but they could not sit in either House of Parliament. As often happens in such cases, partial relief brought no satisfaction, and as the Irish began to see their way into a natural citizenship, they chaffed all the more bitterly against the remaining barriers. Under Thomas Emmet and Robert Emmet, a new sort of struggle arose in Ireland. An appeal was made by eloquence and logic to the feeling of the English people.

Amid a welter of parties supreme efforts were made by the United Irishmen to get the Orangemen and the Defenders to pull together for the relief of Ireland, but the effort was in vain. Tandy, a United Irishman, took the Defenders' oath, was informed against, and was obliged to flee to America. He thus became the hero of the Defenders, but the consequence was the proclamation of the United Irish Society as an illegal organization.

After a brief respite from coercive measures, the law was again strictly enforced and the United Irishmen, despairing of peaceful measures, were reorganized as a secret society with the avowed purpose of separating Ireland from the British Empire. Men of high position, like Lord Edward Fitzgerald, joined the movement. But Emmet was the man of outstanding capacity. Emissaries sent from France, then at war with the Empire, were captured. Jackson was hanged; Tone fled to America. Suspected persons were tortured to secure confessions. Militia were quartered on the wretched peasantry, who were not paid for their unwelcome guests. Tone meantime turning back, went to France and succeeded alone without credentials in securing a French fleet and 10,000 men who sailed from Brest for Bantry Bay in the winter of 1796. The winds had favored William of Orange. They were adverse to the French, who after long effort could not land and returned to France. Another expedition, fitted out in the Texel, failed similarly. At last Tone, whose diary is wonderful reading, was captured and committed suicide.

The following atrocities, and answering atrocities are enough to make angels weep.

The legislative union of Great Britain and Ireland, fostered by Cornwallis, then Lord Lieutenant of Ireland, was carried through by bribery. Peerages were given, English or Irish, in return for votes for the Union.

The union abolished the Irish Parliament, Ireland being thereafter represented in the Imperial Parliament.

Pitt, who had promised Catholic emancipation, suffered the humiliation of having his promise broken by the king.

Among the great names that are blazoned in the skies of Ireland now rises that of Daniel O'Connell, born in County Kerry, near Cahirciveen in 1775. His ability and eloquence made him prominent first as an advocate, and then as a leader in the movement for Catholic emancipation. He founded the Catholic Association. He was sent to Parliament in 1828, was foremost in pressing for "repeal" in 1841, and in promoting mass-meetings, 1842–43. He was arrested in 1843 and convicted of conspiracy and sedition. In 1844 his sentence was reversed. He died in Genoa in 1847. For a long period his influence in Catholic Ireland was almost supreme, and he was loved, even adored, by the mass of Catholic Irishmen.

O'Connell had for a time united Catholic Ireland most compactly. For the first time a great Democratic movement swelled like a tide. Though O'Connell was condemned the Imperial Government passed the Emancipation Bill, and thus was accomplished the contention of O'Connell for the principle of religious equality. Roman Catholics were admitted to Parliament.

While religious and political oppression in Ireland came to an end in the 19th century, the bitterness of the past was not easily eradicated. Under Gladstone a Home Rule bill was carried in the House of Commons but thrown out in the Lords' House. The agitation continued for Home Rule, but when that was obtainable South Ireland desired complete independence. The matter has been settled recently by the separation of Ulster from the rest of Ireland, now established as the Free State. The British Empire retains some isolated naval bases. The Free State has taken over the obligation to settle for the damage wrought to property during the rioting and guerrilla warfare which occurred during the last phase of the contest for freedom.

The republicans stood for the absolute separation of all Ireland from the British Empire. This would have entailed civil war. It was determined by South Ireland, comprising all except six counties of the island, to settle the State on the present basis, thus separating Ulster with its six counties from the Free State. The people of Ulster were as insistent on remaining in the empire as South Ireland was on withdrawing from the empire. A cause of political tension just now is the demarcation of the bounds between the two governments, as the precise county lines are not acceptable to both parties. When and if this difficulty is surmounted there will be brighter hopes of peace than at any previous period. It seems better that the names of persons now living, however illustrious, should not be introduced in an irenic work of this sort, which has nothing whatever to do with political and religious matters.

L'ENVOI

WE LEAVE Ireland with regret but happy in the knowledge that its natural beauties are still there to welcome us again. On the occasion of our next visit we look for more competition, for surely those travelers who seek the charm of unspoiled beauty of nature and instinctive courtesy in people cannot long be kept away from Ireland Beautiful.

ERIN

A land of roses and of rushing burns
And misty vales that shine like silver gauze,
Sweet with the pungence of the fragrant thyme
And bright with rowan trees and scarlet haws;
Purple with heather-bloom and shadowy glens
And rolling wooded hills and mountain-sides;
Green with the shamrock and fair-foliaged trees
Of many a forest where the bluebell hides!
A land that sparkles with a thousand gems,
A myriad of turquoise streams and loughs
Where gamey fish and furry otters dwell
Beneath the boggy braes and hidden rocks;
The River Shannon winding its loved course
From Cuilcagh Mountains to the open sea;
The rough green waters of the seething Moyle
From out its nine glens roaring to be free!
A land whose mountains fringe a ragged coast,
A wild and barren but historic goal,
Whose caves of Rathlin Island sheltered Bruce
And many another lonely driven soul. —
And while the kettles sing upon the hobs
Around the glowing peat weird tales are told
Of the O'Neills, Red Hugh and Owen Roe
And feuds and battles of the days of old.
The land of Erin is enchanted ground
Which left a charm from Hesiod's Golden Race
Within its merry folk of fairy faith,
A charm of love and beauty, wit and grace.
A poem is Erin and a plaintive song
Of passion, sorrow, and adventurous joy;
A fallen monarch's dirge, a mother's croon,
The pipes of Pan, a roaming whistling boy!

Mildred Hobbs

THE MEANING OF IRISH PLACE NAMES

Adare, ford of the oak tree; formerly *Athdara*

Ard, a height or hill, Latin *arduus*

Armagh, *Ard-Macha*, or *Altitudo Machae*, Macha's Height. Macha was a chieftainess

Athlone, *Ath*, a ford. Formerly *Athluain*, the ford of Luan, a man's name

Baltimore, may have been *Beal-ti-mor*, the great habitation of Beal; one of the principal seats of the idolatrous worship of Baal. The old Irish pronunciation was Baile-an-tighe-mhoir, the town of the large house

Bally, town

Ballycastle, originally *Baile-an-chaisil*, town of the cashel. *Cashel* denotes the wall with which the monks surrounded their establishments

Bangor, *Beannchar*, *beann* meaning horns, or pointed hills or rocks; same as *banagher*

Bantry, descendants of the race of Beann

Blarney, *blarna*, little field, from *blar*, a field

Bunratty, the mouth of a river formerly called the Ratty. *Bun*, the end or bottom of anything

Carlow, from *Caherlough*, four lakes. There is a tradition that the Barrow anciently formed four lakes there

Carn, *cairn*, a heap of stones placed over the grave of a person of note

Carrick or *carrig*, rock

Carrickfergus, Fergus's rock.

Carrigadrohid, the rock of the bridge

Carriganass, from *Carraig-an-easa*, the rock of the cataract; takes its name from a beautiful cascade near the castle

Cashel, a wall

Clare, from *clar*, a board, a flat piece of land

Claregalway, *clar*, or *claar*, literally board, applied locally to a plain or flat piece of land

Cong, a narrow strait

Clifden, modern corruption of *clochan,* a beehive-shaped stone house

Clogheen, a place of round stones

Cork, from *corcach,* a marsh

Creagh, an end. Same as *crioch* or *creea*

Derg, red

Derry, doire, or *daire,* oak wood

Donegal, formerly *Dun-na-n-Gall,* fortress of the foreigners

Down, from *dun,* a fort

Downpatrick, a cathedral in County Down, near the place of St. Patrick's first missionary labors

Dublin, formerly *Duibh-linn,* translated black pool; applied originally to the part of the Liffey by which the city is built

Dungory, Guary's fortress. *Dun,* in combinations, generally means fortress

Dunmore, great fort

Fermanagh, from tribe of *Fir-Monach* (*O'Dugan*). The tribe fled from Leinster and settled on the shore of Lough Erne

Gall, a Gaul, hence a foreigner. Used in many place names founded by foreigners

Glengariff, rugged glen

Gweedore, from *gaeth,* sea, and *Doir,* the son of Hugh Allen, king of Ireland, who was slain. *Gaeth-Doir* means Doir's inlet

Inis, island, cognate with Welsh *ynys,* and Latin *insula*

Kenmare, head of the sea; *ceann,* head, and *mara,* sea

Kerry, from *Ciarriadhe,* the race of Ciar, whose descendants possessed a small piece of territory between Tralee and the Shannon

Kildara, cill-dara, the church of the oak

Kill, or *Cill,* church

Killarney, may be from *Cillairneadh,* church of the sloes. *Airne* means sloe bushes

THE OLD PIER—COUNTY CORK

THE GLEN BRIDGE—COUNTY GALWAY

BEHIND THE PALING—NEAR DUBLIN

A PETALED DOOR STEP—ANTRIM   MIDSUMMER BY THE POOL—CORK

A KILLARNEY SHORE—COUNTY KERRY

SHALLOWS OF THE OWENRIFT—COUNTY GALWAY

SHORES OF LOUGH GILL—COUNTY SLIGO

JAMESTOWN GATE——COUNTY LEITRIM

VALLEY COTTAGE——COUNTY KERRY

LEENAUN

Killeedy (County Limerick), the church of Ide, a celebrated nun of the fifth century

Knock, originally *cnoc,* mountain or hill

Kylemore, great wood. *Kyle* in many cases means wood, and *more,* great

Leighlin, half glen

Leitrim, formerly *Liath-dhruim,* gray ridge. *Dhruim* originally meant back

Leixlip, old Norse *Laxhlaup,* salmon leap, so called from the cataract on the Liffey

Limerick, from *Luimneach,* originally applied to a portion of the River Shannon

Lough (Scotch *loch*), a lake or salt water estuary

Lough Finn, lake of Finn

Macroom, crom, bent, inclined; the sloped field or plain, which accurately describes the spot on which the castle stands

Mahee Island, Island of Mochaei, a bishop consecrated by St. Patrick

Mayo, formerly *Magheo* or *Mageo,* the plain of the yews. The county derives its name from a monastery built in the seventh century

Monasterboice, monastery of St. Boethius or Buite, the founder

More, large. Used in many name combinations

Mourne Mountains, from *Mughdhorn,* a tribe of people descended from Colla Meann

Muckross, formerly *Mucross,* from *muck,* a pig, and *ros,* peninsula. *Muckross,* peninsula of the pigs

Newry, anciently called *Iubharcinn-traga,* the yew tree at the head of the strand. Name afterward shortened to *Iubhar,* which, by prefixing the article *an,* was reduced to the present name

Oughterard, from *Uachdar,* upper. *Uachdarard,* upper height

Owenriff, Owan Roimhe, or Brimstone River. *Ruibh* or *roimhe* means sulphur. The river deposits a sulphur scum on the stones in its bed

Portrush, from *Port-ruis,* the landing place of the peninsula

Raphoe Castle, Rath-both, fort of the huts.   *Both* signifies a tent or hut

Roscommon, wood of St. Coman, who founded a monastery there about the seventh century.   *Ros* signifies wood

Ross Castle, from *ros,* a promontory.   (This meaning of *ros* and that above are restricted in point of locality; in the southern half of Ireland *ros* is generally understood in the sense of wood, while in the north it means only a peninsula)

Sligo, named from the *Sligeach,* shelly river

Tipperary, formerly *Tiobrad-Arann,* well of Ara, the ancient territory in which it was situated.   *Tobar,* a well, sometimes called *tipper.*   The well that gave the name to Tipperary was near the main street

Trim, from the elder tree, so called from trees that grew near the old ford across the Boyne

Tuam, called *Tuaim-da-ghualann,* tumulus of the two shoulders, from the shape of the ancient mound here

Tull, a little hill

Tullagh, from *Tulach,* a hill

Tyrone, Tir-Eoghain, Owen's Territory.   Owen was the ancestor of the O'Neills, and his descendants possessed this territory.

Waterford, partly Danish.   The termination *ford* is from *fiord,* and means inlet of the sea.   Called by early English *Badrefiord*

Wicklow, probably Norwegian, called in old documents *Wykynglow, Wygyngelo,* which reminds us of the Scandinavian word *vig,* a bay

INDEX